MIKE AND STEVE SNIEZAK

A Trucker's Survival Guide to Eating In

Commonsense Cooking on the Road

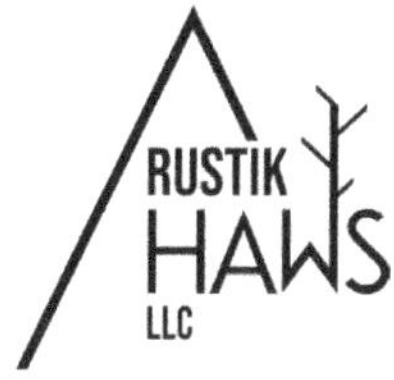

ISBN: 978-1-952244-57-5 (Paperback)
ISBN: 978-1-952244-58-2 (Hardback)
Printed in the United States of America.

Rustik Haws LLC
100 S. Ashley Drive, Suite 600
Tampa, FL 33602
https://www.rustikhaws.com/

TABLE OF CONTENTS

AN INTRODUCTION

M Y NAME IS STEVE Sniezak I am a Chief Steward which is a chef that cooks on ships at sea...and a bit more. I have 30 years cooking experience and 10 years of that has been on high seas from the Bering Sea to the Equator. In addition to that I have been a paramedic, hard hat diver, dive medic, and a hoard of other things...you will find that professional cooks get bored easy. Just the same I am the real deal even though I have never been to one of those fancy cooking schools. I remember while cooking at a Casino in Oregon a culinary student in her last weeks of school was with us for some field training before she graduated. She was assigned to me and we were working in one of the pizza stands on the floor. At one point when things were slow she asked me where I had gone to school. I casually replied that I had never been to a cooking school at which point she put her nose up in the air and with more arrogance then I had seen in some time she says to me, "So you are one of those rouge cooks."...I thought for a few seconds and smiled at her saying, "I like that; yes I am a rouge cook." It has stuck with me ever since so if we ever meet just holler out, "Hay you old rouge cook!" and the first round will truly be on me.

I come from a large family and have three brothers and three sisters. We are all very diverse people truly unique in our own ways and when we all had finally grown past the battles that go with siblings in their youth we found ourselves to be a forceto be reckoned with. When I have trouble with my computer I call brother Don, if it is questions on biology, horticulture, or sanitation brother Larry has it dialed in, Barb is the math guru with no shortage of worldly wisdom, Joan is the baker and has saved my bacon sort of speak more than once. Sister Pat, my mighty Zot is the family counselor which leaves us with Brother Mike…

Brother Mike is a Chief Senior Retired from the Sea Bee's branch of the Navy and if that means anything to you then you already know that Mike or "The Chief" as we call him is the real deal. In the course of this adventure we call life the Chief has raised a brood of children as well as supported more than his share of ex-wives…we call these growing pains. Now with all his duties behind him the Chief is finally doing that which he has always loved. He is driving truck, long haul crisscrossing the country as much as possible and making the cab of his truck his home. For me I call the sea my home but we live for the same thing, to see what is beyond the next horizon.

Thanks to modern technology and a cool little thing called a Blue Parrot Head Set the Chief and I spend a good amount of time on the phone…well whenever I am on the beach. Interesting enough we find that we often talk about food and the difficulties of eating well on the road. One day the Chief called and simply said, "You need to write a cook book." I told him I was and had been for sometime…that's a story for another day. The Chief said, "Not that one, you need to write a cook book for truckers and people who live on the road like we do. You need to teach them how to cook." So here we are, I am at the key board and the Chief is on the road and together we have built test kitchens both here and out there and together we will teach you if you are whiling how to shop, prep, and cook. What equipment to buy and where to buy it. Together we will teach you how to eat healthy and eat well, we will teach you that it is possible to eat three balanced meals plus snacks out of the cab of your truck or in whatever remote position you are in and we will do this for ridiculously little money, because after all other then the adventure that drives us is that not why we are all out there, for the money? If we can save some by learning to eat well is that not worth while? For the record as of this writing in fall 2012 running up and down the left coast the Chief is spending around $10.00 a day for three square meals plus snacks with no need to tip and that is not a misprint. Now keep in mind we are all different and this figure is not a constant but it is do-able and I have fed many a hungry sailor and fisherman for this kind of money and if you know of any they will tell you they do eat well.

The concept of this book is based on the philosophy of my favorite mentor the one and only Johnny Powel Sr. and in Dad's words, "Keep it simple, stupid!" This is exactly what we are going to do. So you will not find fancy French cooking words in here and you will not find the ravings of some fancy chef who is in love with the sound of his own voice. What you will find in here is common sense survival tricks and techniques from as many sources and experiences as I can pack into this little book laid out in a manner that allows you to get your nourishment, stock you pantry, and get on down the road and back to what's important...making those dollars flow.

So enough of this gum flapping, let's get cooking!

DEDICATION

WE AFFECTIONATELY DEDICATE THIS book to Big Bad and my favorite nephew Joe the dog. Big Bad was the Chief's 1989 Ford F-250 heavy duty bought new and recently gave up the ghost on the Oregon state line. Joey was a Border collie who hung with us through thick and thin and when the family was grown and his job done Ole Joey headed on up to heaven where I have no doubt he rides with Big Bad on his special bed in the cab as they chase horizons in heaven the way we do down here. I know it is odd to dedicate a book to a truck and a dog but if you are one of us then you understand and if you don't…you never will.

EASTERN OREGON COWBOY PRAYER

Oh dear Lord, make my food tasteful. Let it stay down
for more than twenty minutes and if it does, please
make a solid turd in the morning.

Amen

EQUIPMENT:

D IFFERENT RIGS, DIFFERENT COMPANIES, different rules...oh my, what do we do? You have to work within the guide lines of your company. Some do not allow elements or open flames, others may not have freezers or only small refrigerators and for the owner operators you guys have enough to think about with fuel costs there is no telling what you have, but you know what it just doesn't matter because ole Uncle Steve and that would be me remembers heating up cans of soup on the exhaust manifold of his 1968 Chevy and opening them up with a P-38 that hangs on my key chain to this day. So let's look at what is out there and then we will address what to do with it.

I will say now and you will hear me say it again, window shopping is very important. I know you budget your money so in the same way budget your time and make sure you leave enough time to shop around for good deals. My favorite example of this is the Waring Waffle Iron, which to me is the finest waffle iron available. When they first came out many years ago my restaurant supply company offered them for $450.00...I found the same model serial number and all at Bed Bath and Beyond for $75.00. So you see it pays to shop around and keep notes if you're serious about finding a deal you will get confused at some point and keeping track of your thoughts, likes, and dislikes can save you money as well.

So where to shop for equipment? First of all the Chief says do not exceed 80% of your inverter. I won't pretend to understand that fully but I don't need to, you do. I know his toaster oven is 110 watts; his microwave is 700 watts both of which are more than enough power to cook quality food. He also has a 4 cup coffee pot, a 3 quart crock pot and a small charcoal grill. I will be using him as our base line because as I said he lives out of his truck so spends more time with her then even a lot of owner operators. So if he can eat happy and healthy then you can too.

If you are limited to or prefer on line purchases, for 12 volt systems go to maxburtonappliances.com I find their prices to be fare and they offer a good variety. They also have cook books for some of their products and I for one like a company that offers something like a cook book for use with their cooking equipment kind of shows they care. Amazon.com is a staple but do not forget they are a warehouse of sorts so some deals are great and some are not. My example of this is the pressure smoker I am currently playing with cost $150.00 at Wal-Mart and $230.00 on Amazon...plus shipping don't forget to factor in shipping and the time you lose waiting for it to get to you. Just the same these are two good on line places to go. You can also window shop Wal-Mart, Costco, and Sam's club on line. Take a moment to search in your area for a wholesale place such as Cash and Carry or United Grocers these are pitched to the restaurant owner but usually sell to the general public as well, if they don't just use your Social Security number as your tax number or I.D. Just the same never leave your calculator at home and look for the unit price. Also do not rule out the dollar stores. There are different kinds some charges a dollar for everything while others do not, so make sure you know which one you are in. Particular equipment deals found in the dollar store are cleaning products and cooking utensils along with plates, cups and glasses.

If you are the kind of person who does not have the time or

interest in shopping around and would rather go to one store then the Wal-Mart super stores are your one stop shopping place period. My 2 quart crock pot cost $10.00 there and I can feed myself with that alone if I wanted to.

MASTER LIST OF EQUIPMENT

Refrigerator, small like 2-4 cubes

Freezer, best to be large like 5 cube if possible

Microwave

Toaster oven

Crock pot 2-4 quart

Coffee pot or electric water pot for boiling water quickly

BUTANE BURNER FOUND AT restaurant supplies, sporting good stores, and on line at either site given. Don't pay more than $30.00 for this and buy one if you can they are very handy. Be careful where you buy fuel for these as this is how they make their money. Truck stops can charge $5.00 a can where as Cash and Carry has them for around $7.00 for a four pack, sporting good stores usually have good prices as well.

If you want a grill for those long 34's Wal-Mart has these cool rectangle charcoal grills which have legs that act as locks for the lid. They are not expensive and do a nice job.

Small meat thermometer, get the kind that can be calibrated. The one I carry is from "The Pampered Chef" model number 2240. These are small and very tough and not very expensive, I am not real current on prices because I usually get mine free from my vendors. Just the same I would not pay more than 10 bucks for such a thing.

2 coffee cups, 2 plates, 2 bowls, 2 forks, 2 spoons, 2 serrated butter knives or strong steak knives

I intentionally put down two of these things for a simple reason, first of all who knows when you will have company and second all these tools will double for other duties. So instead of buying a full set of measuring cups which take up space and have a limited use you have an extra coffee cup which will do just fine for any measuring we need to do.

A small chef's knife the style called Santoku has a rounded nose and is easy to use. Don't buy one longer than 5 inches, there is no point and nothing is worse than a cook with long knife syndrome. Again buy a cheap one; you don't need a hundred dollar knife to survive on the road. Wal-Mart carries a great selection

A nylon style cutting board, small is fine and dollar stores carry these.

A nylon spatula, the kind for flipping hamburgers and eggs, we will use our forks and spoons for any other mixing we need. If you want a ladle or big spoon that's up to you but avoid metal because it rusts and avoid wood because it holds bacteria.

A sauce pot, what I am talking about is something the diameter of a small frying pan but with taller sides and often has a little spout on the rim. Paula Dean's label has a very nice one at Wal-Mart, if possible buy hard anodized instead of Teflon it's a great deal stronger. This is an all purpose pot, with this I can fry eggs or make Mac and Cheese or a hundred other things. Also the Chief tells me that Pilot Truck Stops now carry a 12 ounce, 12 volt, 156 watt, 13 amp Fry Pan for around $25.00. I have not seen this yet but it sounds like a good deal and if the Chief says it is then it is.

This is a lot of equipment so pick and choose what you want or if room allows get it all. I am giving you everything I have what you do with it is up to you, so take your time and read this and research that. In the end it is all about you.

GROCERIES

L ET US START BY packing your reefers and with that a little background Poppa Don the guy that started all this and better known as my Dad was a heating, air conditioning, and refrigeration genius. I knew the fire triangle before I went to kindergarten, so when the Chief and I tell you this is how to pack your reefer and by doing so you will maximize cooling and make your food last longer. Well, you can bet your sweet retreads we ain't just whistling Dixie. Think of the changing conditions in your cab, climbing to elevation, descending to sea level, one minute hot as hell and the next you're reaching for your flannels and now think of your reefers they work by applying pressure to and then releasing inert gasses. They draw moisture out of the air and are a complicated pile of man's attempt to wrestle with heat and cold at the same time. So anything we can do great or small to ease their burden will allow them to run more efficiently, which means the cost of power will be less the food lasts longer and we save more money…anybody starting to see a pattern here?

There are three things to remember when packing your reefer's first is air flow, second cross contamination and third is temperature variation…don't worry it's a lot simpler than it sounds. Air flow is just that each unit requires the air to circulate and spread the cold around. If you have a standing unit like a regular refrigerator or standing freezer then the air flows down the back and as long as there is a gap between your food and the back wall the air will circulate properly. If you have a chest style reefer like the 12 volt ones that look like a cooler then the air flow is across the bottom and all you need to do is leave a channel down the middle when packing it so the air can flow through. Cross contamination is an epic topic that volumes of books have been written on and we simply don't need to be bothered with the bulk of it. So to keep it simple keep anything that is raw and requires cooking to eat and that include eggs away from anything that is cooked or can be eaten raw like lettuce. Put the raw stuff that requires cooking on the bottom so if it drips blood or juice it won't contaminate anything that is cooked or eaten raw like tomatoes. Make sure that the raw bloody stuff is in a sealed package and if possible keep it in your freezer until needed. Which leaves us with temperature variations by which I simply mean heat rises while cold falls so if it requires more cold to stay fresh like raw meat keep it in the bottom while lettuce and such can stay near the top, and if you step back and look at this the three pieces go together to form one well packed refrigerator.

The final thing to note is that reefers are designed to be filled and work better that way. Try to keep yours stocked and rotate your food. It is simple logic to eat the pot roast from last Tuesday before eating the ribs from yesterday. Or to cook the roast that has been thawed for two days before cooking the fish that is still thawing. Also it is an old saying but a good one just the same, "When in doubt throw it out." If you think something has gone bad it probably has and if you have never had any food that has gone bad trust me food poisoning is no fun in the best of circumstances I would hate to be on the road and come down with it.

A couple of things to remember first of all the thing that is generally called an expiration date is not, there simply is no such thing. The date put on certain products is a manufactures recommended used by date. The maker of the product is telling you to use their product before the date given for the freshest taste and cooking results, period. I have seen morons throw away perfectly good milk because it's three days away from the date and turn around and drink sour milk that is new and I could smell the sour from the other side of the room. So a little common sense people that's all I'm asking here.

There is a trick though when shopping, look at the container does not matter if it is a plastic bag or tin can. If the container looks to be swollen then don't buy it, if you take something from your reefer or pantry and that container is swollen don't even open it just throw it away. Trust me if you have ever seen a swollen tin can you will thank me for telling you not to open it. Fermentation is controlled rot, bacteria eat yeast and poop out alcohol, rotten milk is turned to cheese or butter milk or a hundred wonderful things because the bacterium is controlled. If the bacteria is not controlled the result is poison and sickness and the tell tale is the gas given off by all bacteria reactions. Which is what causes the packages can or plastic to swell and if it goes unchecked they will eventually explode.

O.K. then everybody ready to go shopping!?

Buy bulk, buy bulk a shopping we will go. Rule one, every time someone handles a product the price goes up. What is cheaper per pound a steak or a roast? Not the total price the unit price, peeled baby carrots are the bomb and I use them myself but if space allows and you don't mind peeling, a ten pound bag of carrots will last in your home for a long time and save you money…that being said. The peeled baby carrots take up less room and don't require peeling or rinsing. This brings us to rule

   MIKE AND STEVE SNIEZAK

number two and the hardest rule to learn, balance. Is it better for you to buy the ten pounds of carrots or should you go with the 1 pound bag of baby carrots? In the end only you can decide this, in the end when it is you alone out there on the road it truly is all about you but I will give you the tools to make the best choices you can for yourself and more importantly show you how to grow in this area and become your own Chef Hell of the Highway. It tickles me to no end to listen to the Chief go on about some dish he just created or how he and his buddy Eric are swapping recipes and techniques and these guys are manly men there's nothing mushy here. The kitchen is not just for the ladies anymore and there is no reason a man on the road has to live on sandwiches packed by the misses or worse fast food crap that should be outlawed as a general public health hazard! Sorry kind of hit a nerve there, anyway two things to note first off you may have noticed I sort of aim this book at the guys and I know there are a lot of ladies out there hauling loads with the boys and I also know a great deal of ladies that can't cook. The reason I tend to write towards the guys is simply that I am one, I am a man and have no idea how a woman thinks and would not presume to tell a woman how to run her truck anymore then I would tell her how to handle being pregnant. That being said I think there is enough general information here that any lady driver that wants to get better in the eating area can find helpful pointer throughout.

The other thing I will touch on now as long as is has come up is healthy eating, again what you put in your body is up to you I only give you the tools to make healthy choices if you so desire. Also I will give pointers on certain foods that aid in medical areas. I say for the record I am not a doctor and I am not attempting to give medical advice. Also if I give you something that can change your medical profile such as sweet potatoes which reduce the sugar in the body and are a great benefit to diabetics. Not only am I not telling you to go off your medicine and live on sweet potatoes but I am telling you that if you introduce any change like increased sweet potato intake that you discuss this and anything like it with your doctor. Bottom line boys and girls I am a cook and that is all I am and would not prescribe to you medically anymore then I would tell you how to dive your truck…enough on that.

Fast food is crap period; it has been crap for decades and will remain crap until it is outlawed. They can tweak the menus and advertise diet items but in the end it's like trying to put a prom dress on a pig, all you do is waste your time and piss off the pig.

The two killers in our country are salts and carbohydrates… thought I was going to say fats didn't you? Well, fats and sugar are a problem but for them it is more the balance game again.

Salt 101, table salt is a mineral it comes from rocks if you mix table salt in a glass of water it becomes a suspension which means when you stop stirring and put the glass down eventually the salt will separate from the water and settle to the bottom of the glass. We as humans are largely made up of water so what do you think table salt does in us? Just the same salt is needed, in cooking salt opens the tissues of the meat to allow herbs and spices to be absorbed, in the same manor it helps the body absorb the things it needs to absorb. Now let's look at sea salt which is organic, (I apologize this is a very abused word which I avoid like the plague but here it fits) sea salt is made from decomposed animal shells like crabs and shrimp and in water sea salt is a solution which means it mixes in a permanent state…don't believe me go get a glass from the ocean and try to take the salt out if you can figure out an easy way to do that you will be richer then Rockefeller. So for a healthier you the first thing should be replacing table salt with sea salt and before you roll your eyes listen to this. Sea salt is sea salt, I had a nutritionist lecture me once saying that as far as the body was concerned all sugars are the same…I'm still working on that one and I'll get back to you. As for sea salt though once again a fad has been born and I have seen insane types of sea salt for obscene amounts of money…I get mine at the dollar store. It's even cheaper than the grocery store and if you read the label the sea salt at the grocery store has iodine added and the cheap one at the dollar store does not and I don't want iodine added to my sea salt and do you know why I don't want iodine added to my sea salt boys and girls especially when iodine is good for us? BECAUSE IODINE IS NATURALLY OCCURING IN THE OCEANS KELP AND SEA WEED IS PACKED WITH THE STUFF AS IS SEA SALT SO WHY IN GODS NAME WOULD I WANT TO ADD MORE!!?

People that are allergic to shell fish are actually allergic to iodine!

Sorry about that kind of a sensitive area with me but I brought it up to make a point and that is that knowledge is power and the more you know about this stuff the better off you will be to battle the grand marketing machine that has no interest in your health or even your survival but is only interested in making money. This is why I listed salt as a hazard to Americans and why I started here with it. The next time you are in a grocery store start grabbing packages randomly, I do not care what they are just pick them up turn them around and read the salt content which is listed as sodium. The levels are insane, everything has salt added, everything! I picked up a pack of raw beef steaks and they had 5% salt added, RAW! 5% salt added what the hell for?! Well…remember when I told you that salt opens the pores of the meat so we can season it better? When they salt that steak and put it on display the salt opens the pores of the beef and allows the blood remaining to surface which gives it the look we have been conditioned to think of as fresh and inviting…this is a sad state of affairs indeed and if you are in a position where you can buy you meat bulk or from a professional old world style butcher shop and if bless your heart you are a hunter or fisher and can stock your freezer at home with wild game that is the best first thing you can do for a healthier life.

Carbohydrates, breads, flours, starches, grains…very, very important part of what we are and very misunderstood and subsequently abused by most of us, First of all if any of you live by the food pyramid throw that P.O.S.. away. We are individuals and have individual needs and no one structure can guide us all. Carbohydrates are the energies that drive us, but need to be burned off quickly. If not burned off they turn to sugars which turn to fats and if you stop on any street U.S.A. and look around you at the obesity, if you yourself as a truck driver sitting behind the wheel for all those long hours battle with being overweight then carbohydrates and the fast food empire is a good place to start. My first exposure to this was on the Bering Sea feeding processors, generally young kids fresh in the world looking for fast money and adventure…they found the money if they survived it but the adventure was a cold dark, world of nonstop back breaking work the like of which most people could not even wrap their minds around and my job was to keep the machine running. Keep the processors fueled up with all the energy we could to keep them working and we did this by increasing their carbohydrate intake. A balanced meal on a ship consists generally of two entrees two vegetables and a starch. For the processors we added another starch to each meal and then made

Carbohydrates available for snacking. This is where you found the chips and popcorn various health bars loaded with carbs. What was fascinating is most of the guys that came out there lost weight and increased muscle tone and were pretty damn tough when they left because the carbohydrates were being used quickly and efficiently. Now let's go to your truck, you grab a breakfast sandwich from a fast food place the stuff they call meat on it has been fluffed with some kind of grain or flour or other starch to bulk it up and increase the profit margin, it's on a big fat piece of bread to make it look more presentable and comes with a side of fried potatoes… actually the greasy potatoes are the only good part because the grease causes the pyloric valve in the stomach to open and gets that crap you just ate out…same concept as greasy fries on a hangover. So down the road you go many hours until your first stop and although I do not mean to belittle and have nothing but admiration for the people that haul goods in our country. For the next few hours you are sitting behind a wheel, mental energy yes…physical energy…not so much and anything you just ate that has any connection with a starch or carbohydrate just settled into your belly and hips and the lining of your veins and arteries…with me so far. So what do we do? Simple again, knowledge is power and you just learned what has been causing your weight problems all these years, so does that mean you must live on tofu and bean sprouts? I certainly hope not because they are both Carbohydrates. We will get into this all in greater detail when we get to the cooking part but here for an overview, how about start by losing the bread? Buy the egg, sausage, cheese thingy but peel off the bread and toss it you don't need it. Here's another trick, in the cultures that eat real spicy food you see less obesity…ever wonder why? The spice will have a chemical reaction similar to the physical reaction of working hard, peppers burn fat, which uses carbohydrates.

Now don't think if you munch a jar of jalapeños everyday you will look like Twiggy by May, not only will that not work but you are only lying to yourself. Just the same a diet, (Oh and diet does not mean fad or starving or stupid shit like that diet means living healthy and eating well) that included hot peppers is a wonderful way to keep your blood healthy and clean. Cayenne is best but any hot pepper is good, also raw garlic is very good for you as it reduces blood pressure and is a natural anti-biotic. The hick up with garlic is that when you heat it you kill the beneficial properties. So if you are like I am and love to cook with garlic or find that raw garlic is too strong for you to eat. Then buy granulated garlic, not garlic powder and never garlic salt! Granulated garlic is pressed and dried and not heated so I use it as a condiment like you would salt and pepper, also if you use cayenne pepper in the same way you can start with a very small amount and over time you will get used to it the neat thing about cayenne is that in small amounts it is a flavor enhancer which means if you put a little on your food you taste more food without tasting the pepper but remember start small.

A side note; looking over what I have written so far it is easy to think I promote being cheap and in reality I am anything but. I have very pricey toys and enjoy them greatly. So let's take a moment to clarify what it is I am saying and I can think of no better way than to quote the late great Chef Ramón Simbeck a man to great to put into words who gave me the knowledge and the courage to be what I am today. So as the Chef would say, "You only need two things to have a successful restaurant. One, you have to have fun, if you are not having fun you don't need to be there, and two. Buy the very best ingredients that you can afford."

Get it, the best that you can afford and by knowing that you can

                                    Mike and Steve Sniezak

save money by buying sea salt at the dollar store that gives you more money to buy a better cut of meat for that next 34 and a day with the grill. Also understanding how things are sold, beef tenderloin is where they get file' minion, the file' may cost $10.00 for a 8 oz. cut while the tenderloin can be found on sale for around $5.00 a pound which is a savings of 75%! Even if you don't trim the tenderloin and unless I have a lady over I don't and just toss it on the grill with a little wood chip and a light rub...honey hush! Tell me it's not worth buying cheap ass salt and stuff to afford that every once and awhile!?

The Chef was also right about having fun, if you really want to enjoy what this book has to offer and get healthy along the way you have to start with that thing between your ears. You must be positive about committing yourself to shopping, prepping, and cooking, and have as much fun as you can. I know there are lonely days out there, they are there for us all but just think like you are at a tail gate party the next time you're on a long 34 and if you just have fun by yourself believe me it won't be long before the world is knocking on the door of your cab wanting to know why...the world hates being left out of fun.

Back to grocery shopping; you may have noticed that I am not telling you what food to buy that would just be nuts. I'm here to show you how to buy, starting with when. If you and your schedule allow grocery shop at a 24 hour store in the middle of the night this gives you time to think about what you are doing but for most of us this is just not possible or desirable. Sunday during church is a good time to shop or if you happen to be in church then right after is good because most people will be going to Sunday brunch or heading home to relax and get ready for the week. Sunday afternoon is alright but you should avoid the super stores as there will be many people out Sunday window shopping just not for food. Monday morning works as well because most people will have done their shopping on Friday or Saturday and are now starting their week. The neat thing about your job is you are not a true 9-5 kind of person the down side is you all run different schedules so just plan for the best time that works for you remembering that most of America does their grocery shopping on Saturday morning so that's when the stores are crowded.

Read the labels, watch sodium levels, buy raw vegetables or frozen. Canned vegetables are just packed with salt, in all honestly if I could not travel with fresh or frozen vegetables I would probably do without, so do what you can to avoid the cans. As for the frozen vegetables most are pretty high in salt as well but I have found a few that seem to be more realistic in this area and one is a company called "Pictsweet" they advertise flash freezing their vegetables on or near the farms and the ones I have bought were around 1% sodium and that's about as salt free as you will get. Also a company out of Georgia called "Fresh Frozen"; I like these guys because their bags are clear so you really see what you are buying and the field peas with green beans I bought last night had no salt at all added…I had to read the bag twice to believe it! You want to know how bad this salt thing is start reading labels on salt free products…they got sodium in them…yup, yup, yup…Wal-Mart carries both brands and also some of the Wall-Mart brand of vegetables are low in salt as well, some of them. Always read the labels and leave yourself enough time to do so calmly if you are in a hurry you will eat crap all week. When you are making your shopping list at home focus on products that can be used in multiple ways. For instance there are two groups of vegetables that are used so often they have been given fancy French names "Trinity" which is bell peppers, onions, and celery is a main ingredient in such things as Gumbo. While "Mirepoix" is carrots, celery, and onion and is the basic starting ingredient for soups and stews and I apologize for using fancy cooking words after I said I wouldn't, let's just call this one time an occupational hazard. So, list products you will use in multiple ways. Are you going to make soup this week and if so how many times? Will there be stews or roasts and vegetable sides as well? How many carrots do you need per meal? Around 4 ounces of vegetable per meal is what is taught, in reality we eat around 8 ounces and if you are a big person you will need more. Just the same a one pound bag of baby carrots should make one soup, one stew, one side vegetable, and have enough for a salad…possibly two. So one bag of baby carrots can feasibly be an ingredient in four meals, so two pounds of baby carrots would be enough for a 7 day work week plus a day for cushion. These are averages not gospel chiseled in stone, cooking is the knowledge of a base line it is not an exact science and anyone who tells you different is a moron. I used to be terrified of baking, to me it was an exact science and all the precise measurements scared the crap out of me. Until I found myself in a position where it was a part of my job and I had no choice. So by being forced to bake I embraced it and in time found there wasn't that much exacting about it… just understanding and if you ever want to be the Captain of a starship you need to understand how shit works. Later I will give you a recipe for basic bread that is so simple it should be illegal, and you can bake it in your toaster oven or if all you have is a crock pot you can even bake it in that. Can you imagine driving down the road and having the cab of your truck fill with the smell of homemade bread, and for a few pennies a loaf!

This part of the book is more for the people that get to go home occasionally and have a home where they can prepare products and possibly meals for the road. If you are one of the ones living on the road or not having a home to go to then this bulk stuff is not for you, don't worry though most of this book is written for you and those that go home can use what follows to organize their pantries.

Prime rib, you can pay $80.00 for one of these things and what is one person going to do with this big ole thing out on the road? Well…On average you get about 20 steaks from one prime which comes out to $4.00 a steak for Rib eye steak… where are you going to go out to eat and find a price like that? Better yet go look at the Rib eye cuts in the store and see if you can find one for $4.00. In certain places you can find 50 pound bags of flour for under $10.00 while 1 pound bags can be $1.00 or more, so you can buy bulk for a fifth of the price. These are just examples most of you won't need 50 pounds of flour…just the same if you can store it and you do use it for baking and roux's for gravy and thickening soups and stews. Well it is something to think about and as for storing flour it just needs somewhere cool and dry and if you are concerned about bugs getting into it, pickle buckets work nice as well as rolling carts that are designed for such things and also mix some whole bay leaves in the flour it keeps the bugs out and adds a pleasant fragrance to the room. Rice and pasta can also be bought bulk and stored easily enough, again store them with whole bay leaves mixed in. A weevil is a little pain in the ass that is small enough to eat through a plastic bag without being noticed until your bags of pasta have turned to weevil poop and dust…they are to me a plague on ships, but the little fellows hate bay leaves. The choices are yours just remember the more bulk you can buy and store the less often you need to go shopping and the more time you can spend living life when not on the road. I am also a fan of vacuum sealing systems you can take one of those steaks we talked about, seal it in plastic double wrap it in freezer paper and it will last for years frozen if necessary, freezer burn is basically dehydration run amuck so keeping frozen stuff sealed in air tight packages is important. Keep your herbs and spices simple again trying to buy the ones you like the most and can use on many different products; fresh herbs are nice and make your cab smell good but if you cross state lines often this may be an issue to avoid, granulated garlic, sea salt, cayenne pepper, paprika, white pepper, nutmeg, and basil are an awesome base line. You will also need baking soda, baking powder, flour, corn meal if you are into corn bread, and yeast for baking. Luxury items if you have the room would be cream of tartar and buttermilk. Note I left out black pepper, I do this because black pepper gets hotter the longer it cooks so is an unstable element in dishes that cook while you drive and black pepper is also very hard on the stomach lining. I keep it on the tables at work for a condiment but other than that I rarely cook with black pepper anymore.

Another thing to consider are rubber gloves the nitrile ones are best, latex can cause rashes and if you happen to be allergic latex gloves will mess you up, I try not to use them also stick with powder free gloves the ones with powder just make a mess. The environment you work in on the road is not very clean I have the same problem on the ships at sea. Steal boxes packed full of strangers from all points of the planet. So it is deadly serious for me to keep things as clean as possible fortunately for me I have running water, you do not. Gloves help to eliminate the need to wash your hands as often although I cannot stress enough to wash them as much as possible. Keep a small spray bottle of distilled water around it will come in very handy, you can use it to rinse your hands as well as rinse off dishes and utensils after using them. The Chief started carrying distilled water on his truck because he smokes a cigar every now and then and this is the water used in humidors. He found soon enough that he uses distilled water in a great many ways and sure you can cook with it why not? At less than $1.00 a gallon it's a good way to save some money unless you are a water nut and have to have fancy water which is generally city water that has been filtered an extra time…Small spray bottles can be found at the dollar stores. Buy an all purpose degreaser and disinfectant, the 409 brand is my favorite and it kills E coli don't use bleach it is a dinosaur from another time and is no longer needed and is far too dangerous to be used by anyone not professionally trained to understand it. Don't even use it on your whites there are enough product choices to not have to bleach anything anymore.

Alright, well I think we did a pretty good over view the details will work themselves out as we journey forward. Just remember to keep it simple, structure your time and take notes. You are no stranger to a log book well maybe you should keep a log book for your eating. Menu plans, shopping lists, price comparisons, store comparisons, good recipes, mistakes made, (and yes I still make them) and receipts for your accountant at tax time presented with a box of your homemade cookies might go along ways…

BREAKFAST

I WAS WORKING A SALMON camp in Alaska a few years back; college kids from all over Europe came there on work/tourist visas. There were also American college kids there for some summer time money, so ole Uncle Steve got to do some cultured comparisons. For three months breakfast was always the same, an hour before work started the European kids would start to trickle in. They would quietly wander about rubbing the sleep from their eyes, nibbling on bread and fruit, sipping coffee or tea and basically enjoying the morning. A half hour before work started they would wonder off to get ready for the job and fifteen minutes before the job started they were lined up in front of the time clock chatting about home and friends and getting mentally prepared for the day ahead...five minutes go by...ten minutes go by, and BAM!! Here come the Americans like a herd of cattle stampeding through my galley! Stuffing cereal, bacon, eggs, grease, grease, carbs, and grease washing it down with scalding coffee and racing off to the time clock hoping not to be late and pulling up their pants and buttoning their shirts along the way!

It's o.k. to laugh, I did every morning and the Europeans were in constant awe.

Just the same what do you think the American's did to their bodies? Shocking them awake, going from sleep to running wide open without giving their systems time to adjust, stuffing grease, carbs and crap down their throats barely chewing and gulping it down like big fat birds…and you wonder why America is out of shape. I was like that once, I am no stranger to the fast track American life style but fate gifted me. My first ship at sea and a life time of rushing to the time clock now I found I lived on the job and the office was at the end of the hallway… and often I was still late. For me this was unacceptable. So I started getting up earlier five minutes, ten minute, fifteen…still was not working, screw it! I started getting up an hour early and you know what friends and neighbors, I like it! I lived in a world where the office was at the end of the hall and I was getting up for work an hour early and it was awesome! I would go make a light breakfast, get my bucket of Joe, say hay to my friends and often wander back to my room to collect my thoughts and prepare for the day. You see the bottom line is if you don't start out the day on a run chances are you won't have to run through your day.

Also look at the diet differences the European kids were eating fruit, yogurts, teas, smoked salmon, and breads. The Americans were focused on sweets and proteins if they used carbs they were sweetened, so by half way through the day the Americans were dragging and used lunch to recharge which meant by dinner they were waking up which meant they stayed up later then they should have and started the next day dragging where as the others were balanced in their diet and got up early, went to bed early and had a more productive day which is why they were hired for these jobs and most Americans were not.

Balance people the universe demands it and if you do not give balance to the universe the universe will take it from you.

My challenge of balance is how to give you fast food that is good for you, let's give it a try.

　　　　　　　　　　MIKE AND STEVE SNIEZAK

Micro wave 101, a micro wave no matter how strong or weak has a penetration of approximately two inches. This is why if you have ever cooked something of size in a micro wave the outside is often over cooked while the inside can be cold or raw. This is also why they have turn tables in them to expose as much of whatever it is to the beams of radiation. So how you place what you want to cook in a micro wave is important.

Egg note; Most people say an egg will explode in the micro wave and I have seen this happen. I have also made very nice sunny side up eggs this way; it's only a matter of practice. So if you like your eggs hard and don't care for a runny yolk then break the yolk with a tooth pick or knife tip before you cover the plate, if the yolk is broke it will not explode. The white of the egg will pop a bit which is one reason it is covered by cling wrap. Also a little water on the plate like a teaspoon full will sort of steam things and keep everything cooking even. I don't use this in this recipe because you live in an environment where water is hard to come by and it really is not all that important for this. What is important is to realize that once you get things cooking they will tend to keep cooking so rather than micro waving breakfast until it's reduced to raw carbon…cook it a little under and let it stand for a few minutes. Not only is it cooling it is completing its cooking or as we in the cook show say, "It be resting".

While breakfast is resting you could be making coffee…again balance your time.

THE THREE MINUTE BREAKFAST

Take a micro wave safe plate and spray it lightly with a can spray, (a dollar store item). Crack two raw eggs in the middle of the plate, place three raw sausage links around the outside, (frozen links work just fine). Wrap top of plate with plastic wrap, the kind that is called "cling", set a frozen premade biscuit on top of plastic covered plate and micro wave for three minutes or until sausage is heard to sizzle and eggs are done to your liking. Careful plate maybe hot...duh...

Add a little butter and, or honey to your biscuit or cream cheese. With a cup of black coffee and some juice of choice and this is as close to a healthy breakfast as we get in America. A couple of notes, I intentionally said butter and not margarine or a blend which are all crap and should be outlawed. Any spread other than real butter is hydrogenated which means it will plug up your arteries faster than a groupie will jump a rock star. So eat butter or do without, black coffee folks or maybe with honey, Stevia, or Splenda anything else is a death wish. If you must use cream then use something of quality like half and half and stay away from premade creamers...just reading the labels makes me ill. Good pure juice the rest are sugar water flavored with fruit, personally I would rather just have a piece of fruit.

EUROPEAN BREAKFAST

1 fresh croissant with a bit of soft butter, honey, or jam, 1 cup black coffee, about 2 ounces of smoked salmon, three fat strawberry's, two slices of melon of choice, and a banana, possibly a cup of apple juice.

Don't knock it until you have tried it.

BREAKFAST CHIEF STYLE

The Chief starts his week during his 34, this is where he's doing laundry, maybe some shopping to refresh supplies and preparing his week. The egg dish I gave you and others can be a bit messy and for the Chief he does not want to waste time in the morning and would rather be driving. So on Sunday he will hard boil 6-12 eggs, this way he has a hardboiled egg with breakfast every morning and some for salads and stuff. Simply put as many whole eggs as you want into a pot like the one I mentioned in the equipment section, fill pot with water enough to just cover the eggs. Put pot on a burner, if you are on the road this is where that butane burner comes in handy if at home just use your stove. Bring the water to a boil for about 5 minutes. Take the pot off the heat and set it somewhere safe to cool. Whenever you do something like this take a moment to be sure your hot pot will not hurt anyone where it is sitting, trip hazards are one of the greatest dangers in a professional kitchen, and in your cab they can be very costly. Now simply allow the eggs in water to cool this will take a while but when they are cool to the touch then they are ready to peel, eat or store.

If you can't boil water on the road and have a coffee pot make a pot of hot water and pour it over room temperature whole eggs and let them cool, not the best way to cook an egg but we do what we must.

Equipment note; If you are not allowed an open flame in your cab, I suggest a small rice cooker. They are common at places like Wal-Mart and cost no more than our small crock pots. The one I use comes with a rack just for hard boiling eggs, and steaming vegetables, but be aware the outside of these get considerably hotter than a crock pot so again be careful where you put it...

burning down your cab is no fun for anyone.

The Chief has gotten around the peeling of the egg hassle of which I could write a book alone about and he simply cracks the hardboiled egg in half and eats it with a spoon, the simplest answers are always the best.

A typical breakfast for the Chief is 1 hardboiled egg, two links of turkey sausage, 1 Sunny Delight, and a cup of Tully's French Roast coffee. To many of you these sound like a snack and there was a time I would agree, but this is actually a balanced and healthy breakfast which will not weight you down or slow you down. I suggest strongly that you use it as a base line to get yourself going in the morning. Also you want to eat about five times a day but small amounts. What this does is keeps the metabolism going so the motor is always idling, always burning fuel and never just sitting and getting fat.

So, my thoughts on this are to combine what we have seen. Nuke you breakfast meat of choice, (micro waved bacon is considered a very healthy way of preparing bacon) along with a frozen biscuit. Peel a hardboiled egg, have your coffee and a piece of fruit and down the road you go.

Health note; If you do not do tea and wish to get off the coffee but need that morning pick up then mix one tablespoon of honey and one tablespoon of apple cider vinegar into a glass of water. Don't worry, it tastes a lot better than it sounds and is a healthy energy drink. I have made it by the gallon for long hauls.

Also we cannot say enough about oatmeal, it is insanely healthy for you and I highly recommend a bowl a day but in all honesty I think it tastes like paste and would rather plug my pipes then suffer a life of oatmeal. If you have to fill your bowl with brown sugar and stuff just to get it down then just stop because you are defeating the purpose and killing yourself with more sugar. Which brings up another point, within reason eat stuff that makes you happy, oatmeal makes me gag so how can it be beneficial to me personally if I dread eating it? Don't force yourself to eat things because they are good for you, you simply are covering yourself in negative thoughts and not doing a thing for yourself. Bananas have everything in them you need to live and you could survive on bananas alone rather well, Kiwi fruit is in the same family but has more potassium then a banana. Potassium is a chemical that helps the body with electric movement, (sort of keeps your battery terminals clean where the cables connect). Cut a Kiwi fruit in half or cut off the top and scoop it out with a spoon to eat it, just like with the hard boiled eggs. If you have trouble with leg cramps or cramps in general you probably need more potassium and should eat more bananas or kiwi fruit. In an emergency a glass of Gatorade will remove cramps very quickly. A sweet treat is a banana dipped in peanut butter and then drizzled with honey. This is very good for you and will give you a damn good rush! One last thought on oatmeal and this is purely a personal opinion…most cholesterol medicines are taken in the evening or before bed so they can scrub the cholesterol out of you arteries while you rest or sleep. Oatmeal does basically the same thing so I would think it would be healthier to eat a bowl of oatmeal in the evening or as a snack before bed. Also for those of us on such medicine, (never said I was an angel) we know that while taking them you must not have any grapefruit or grapefruit juice it sort of intensifies the cholesterol medicine. So for those of you that are not taking cholesterol medicine it might be a good idea to increase the amount of grapefruit or grapefruit juice you consume and yes leave the damn sugar off of it. Once again I am not a doctor and do not play one on TV, this last section in particular is my opinion drawn from time and experience and I strongly recommend you talk over any great life changes in diet, (remember what I said that was) with your doctor and do not make radical changes in your life, baby steps, always baby steps.

Our diets are high in acid while our bodies are highly alkaline… cosmic humor never gets old. Lemons, watermelon, and strawberry's are some of the highest alkaline foods, try to eat some of these daily.

The next time you get acid gut from too much coffee or pizza try munching a few strawberry's or a piece of watermelon and see how fast it goes away…kind of awesome really.

PIGS IN A BLANKET

I have always thought of these as a snack or lunch food but I have come to respect them for breakfast as well. Later on I will give you a recipe for fresh bread and the dough from that works for these as well, but for breakfast let's cheat a bit.

Get a tube of those raw biscuits, buy the no name ones they are half the price of the name brand and a biscuit is a biscuit. If you want to make your own go to the baking section of this here book.

You will also need some little smokies or a small sausage like that; you can also cut any sausage to that size. Some American cheese and some sliced pickled Jalapeno peppers, (this is the healthy part because they make you sweat but feel free to leave them out if you don't like them).

Take a raw biscuit and gently stretch it out a little like it was a small pizza. Take a half slice of cheese and lay it on the flat biscuit, then a couple of pieces of jalapeno, and finally a sausage. Wrap or roll the biscuit around the other stuff and kind of pinch the edge together.

Make as many of these as you want, place them seam side down on a cookie sheet and bake them in your toaster oven at 350 degrees for about 20 minutes or until they are golden brown and you see a little cheese bubbling out. Bake by smell, trust your nose and don't become a slave to a kitchen timer. Remember we can always add more heat but we can never take it away.

You can also make these up in advance and freeze them; you don't need to thaw them out just straight from freezer to oven and it will only take an extra five to ten minutes baking time for the frozen ones.

If you can't have a toaster oven in your rig you can make these up in bunches at home, bake them and then freeze them. A couple of minutes in the micro wave and you are good to go, they can be baked in your crock pot as well just spray the pot with pan spray and line the bottom with these but plan on a few hours to bake them…unless you really love these I would not recommend the crock pot. My point is don't be afraid to improvise, that is after all what made America great in the first place.

CALIFORNIA OMELET

There is a type of omelet made in California that is not folded. Pretty much it is scrambled eggs with cheese on top, but some big wig chef out there gave it some fancy name and fu-fu whatever was born...don't ask me folks it's California. Just the same it's a cool micro wave breakfast.

Dice up a shot glass full of onion...hell dice up the whole thing and put the rest in a sandwich bag in the refrigerator we will use it, do the same with a bell pepper, a tomato and some mushrooms. Putting about a shot of each into a micro wave bowl like a soup or cereal bowl, Chunk in some ham if you want, how much? I don't know how hungry are you? Hit it with a tablespoon of butter, cover it and nuke it for 1 minute. Take two or three eggs, (how hungry are you?) and when the micro wave pings break the eggs into the hot stuff in the bowl and using your fork mix it all together, it does not need to be even or pretty or fancy because next you will sprinkle shredded cheese on top which will hide everything anyway...what kind of cheese? What kind you got? See y'all; fancy chefs become fancy chefs by deciding these things for you...think about it. Now it's time for you to be the chef hell of the highway and pick your own cheese!

Cheddar is most common.

Cover it back up and nuke it for two minutes more or until the eggs stops running and breakfast is yours, oh and change this in any way you want after all it is your breakfast not mine...I'm kind of a Mimosa or Bloody Mary breakfast kind of guy myself... actually that's how I got my first A.K. 47... Thanks Barb.

BISCUITS AND GRAVY

Often sought after, sinfully simple, a Southern staple.

Take enough ground sausage of choice, (Italian rocks and Jimmy Dean is the bomb) to fill your hand, about the size of a hard ball from your baseball days. Break this up into a fry pan or pot or whatever you got. As it is heating up chunk in a big fat spoonful of butter, a pinch of sea salt, and a dash of cayenne pepper, stir and cook this until the sausage is all brown and broken up and there is a bunch of oil and stuff in the pot. Now mix in about three good teaspoons (which is actually 1 tablespoon) of flour, what you want is a wet paste with all the flour mixed into the meat. Then pour in a cup of milk, just fill your clean coffee cup with milk and pour her in keep mixing until you have nice creamy gravy. If it's too dry add more milk, if it's too wet let it cook a while to thicken up. Add salt and pepper to taste and after your biscuits are done have at it!

Take two of those raw biscuits we talked about, or your own made if you wish, (in the baking section of this book). Put them on a cookie sheet and bake them in your toaster oven for around 7 minutes or until G.B.D. (golden brown and delicious).

Gravy options

This comes from Fred who you will meet later when we get to snacks and stuff, she (Fred) is an old friend from…well as she would put it, "The Low Country" and brings with her a unique perspective to life. Fred says this is best made in a cast iron skillet and I agree…but for us on the road such things can be luxury. I grew up in a cast iron world and would not want to live without it but it takes understanding we don't have time to teach you right now just the same if you have cast iron knowledge, (you probably don't need this book) and a butane burner more the better.

Tennessee Tomato Gravy, fry up some bacon in a pan about four strips, you can break up the bacon and leave it in the gravy or remove it what we need is the grease. As an option you can also sauté in some of those diced onions we stuck in the sandwich bad in the fridge, sauté only means roll them around in the pan a bit until they get kind of clear looking and with practice this can be done in the microwave just remember to cover it so it does not splatter the inside of said microwave. Again add a few spoons of flour just enough to make a wet paste and then add milk, around a cup to get your basic gravy. Now Fred says to mix in as many crushed tomatoes as you can at this point but if we are doing this on the road then keeping a can of crushed tomatoes may not be an easy thing to do but we do have diced tomatoes in the fridge left over from that weird omelet and if not we can dice a bunch up cause we will use fresh tomatoes in a bunch of different things where as canned tomatoes are only good for sauce and stuff...get it? So at this point mix in as many diced, sliced, chunked or what have you tomatoes you got laying around and cook this until it is to your liking. Then add sea salt and cayenne pepper to your taste and over the biscuits it goes. This is also real good on mashed potatoes, or left over mashed potatoes that you just fried in the pan for breakfast, or maybe potato pancakes which we will get to in a minute.

Fred is a vegetarian and I feed people like her all the time and it really is not a big deal and I think this gravy is a good example of why. I try to tailor this book for everyone and if you are a vegetarian there is plenty in here for you. To make tomato gravy for a vegetarian simply replace the bacon and bacon grease with butter or vegetable oil enough to make a puddle in the bottom of the pan about ½ inch deep, the rest remains the same...you see no big deal.

Canola Oil; Again my attitude protrudes, got it from my father or at least the German part of him. I do not use canola oil and many people that study such things are still on the fence when it comes to is this good stuff or bad stuff…I look at it like this. Canola stands for Canadian Oil and is oil pressed from a seed known as the rape seed. Canola was originally used as machine oil…get it, this was Canada's version of Liquid Wrench…and now we eat it…gives me the Willie's but if it don't bother you then party on.

PANCAKES

Electric pan, or butane burner if you don't have some kind of grill top or pan then the best thing to do for pancakes is to make them at home and freeze then, seal as many as you want in vacuumed plastic and microwave them on the road or buy the pre made ones.

There is a recipe in the baking section of this book but in all honesty I recommend a mix like the one Krusty makes and if you want to do some road side baking then the Bisquick mix can give you biscuits, pancakes, cinnamon buns, (awesome recipe on the box!) and other things as well. If pancakes and waffles are your thing then Krusty's is what you want. What is the difference between a pancake mix and a waffle mix? Oil and egg, that's it make enough pancake batter for about four good sized pancakes add one egg and around 1/8 cup of vegetable oil and you have waffle mix. We won't cover waffles on the road because I haven't found an iron I like for that yet but if you want to do them at home then Waring Waffle irons are the best bar none and Bed Bath and Beyond usually carries them for a good price.

If you have a grill surface, fry pan, or such then pour about a cup or two of the pancake mix into a bowl and slowly add enough water to make a wet paste like the mud you would mix to plaster a wall or that mud puddle mud you truck through in the hills during hunting season...you may have noticed I really don't measure much and rather then get your cab full of measuring tools and scales and crap I figure teaching you my way is cheaper for you.

O.K. then, trick number one if you want your pancakes to be thick and fluffy leave the batter a little lumpy. If you beat the dog crap out of it you will make crapes which are French fu-fu pancakes and all the other truckers will laugh at you so please just don't go there! The oil in a pan is what makes the swirl marks on a pancake so less oil makes a prettier pancake but if you're on the road, who care?

Trick two when you see bubbles in the pancake it is time to flip it, pancakes that are thick cook slow so don't have the heat to high half way is a good place to start. The pancake is done when you gently thump the middle and it does not feel squishy.

Options, add some vanilla about half a teaspoon it's pretty strong, a pinch of cinnamon and nutmeg into the batter makes a nice pancake. Chopped pecans are great, as are frozen or fresh blueberries (dry ones don't work well). Chocolate chips are great for the kid in all of us...how much of any of these... about a hand full in the batter is enough for four pancakes or so. I tend to overdue the amount of nuts and things because breakfast cereals never do and I was pissed off as a kid and still am...I mean where are the marshmallows anyway!

Potato Pancakes, either left over mashed potatoes that you turn into soup with some milk and then mix in pancake mix to get the batter you need, or make a wet pancake batter and stir in instant mashed potatoes to get the batter thick enough, mix this with sautéed onions and some bacon bits and grill as you would a normal pancake.

FRENCH TOAST

Traditionally a way to use stale bread French toast is what we call an egg wash I now give you three options.

1.) Traditional; 3 eggs, ¼ cup of cream or whole milk, ¼ teaspoon of cinnamon, ¼ teaspoon vanilla, 1 teaspoon sugar. Whip mixture together, dip slices of bread into it one at a time coating them well place on hot greased griddle, or frying pan until brown about 3 minutes, turn and repeat, remove and eat. Makes about 4 slices.

2.) High End; the milk was added to the traditional mix because it was cheaper than the eggs and was used to stretch the mix. For a better quality toast, break 5 eggs and leave out the cream, the rest remains the same.

3.) U.S. Toast, (that would be Uncle Steve or me); 3eggs broken in a bowl, add ¼ cup of fresh orange juice, ½ teaspoon cinnamon, ½ teaspoon nutmeg, ½ teaspoon vanilla. The rest remains the same

This wraps up breakfast although there will be things throughout the rest of the book that may inspire your creative genius which is really what it's all about. I would like to close this section with something near and dear to my heart. I would not try this on the road or at least not yet but at home on the weekend with the one you love…why not?

The book I sell to you, my personal Benedict recipe…that be a gift.

EGGS BENEDICT

Is a dish where a toasted English muffin is covered by a slice of Canadian bacon, a poached egg, and Hollandaise sauce. Two of these are a single order; to make this traditional dish simply follow what follows but leave out the seafood mix, and as your eggs are poaching, grill four slices of Canadian bacon and toast two buttered English muffins on the grill; this only takes a few minutes. Place bacon on the muffin, egg on the bacon, sauce on the egg and enjoy.

CREOLE BENEDICTS FOR TWO

Start by filling a two quart pot half way full of water and adding ¼ cup of white vinegar. Place pot on the stove to boil.

Find a metal bowl just large enough to cover the pot of boiling water without touching the water, into this bowl place the yolks of four eggs, (to separate eggs crack the shell on a counter corner, break shell into two pieces over the sink, keep the egg in one half, gently pour the egg yolk into the other half shell allowing the white of the egg to fall away to the sink…we don't need it.) a tablespoon of lemon juice, a tablespoon of water, pinch of sea salt and dash of cayenne pepper.

In a micro wave safe bowl melt ½ pound, (2 sticks) of butter and set aside.

In a small sauce pan sauté in a tablespoon of butter the following, one cup of chopped crawfish, or shrimp, or any combination of sea food you enjoy. Generally I do this with crawfish, a little sea salt, and a dash of cayenne pepper, pinch of thyme leaves, pinch of oregano and a little nutmeg. Once this is all bubbly and nice looking hit it with a splash of nice white wine (about 1 shot), stir it well and set it off to the side.

With the water boiling and holding the metal bowl with a towel or over mitt set it on top of the pot of water stirring constantly but slowly, as the egg yolk mix begins to get hot slowly pour in the butter a little at first and then gradually more continually stirring, (a whisk works best) until you have a nice thick sauce. This is more art than science and may take some practice so don't try it on your sweetie until you have made it for yourself. Once you have a nice creamy sauce set it off to the side. If it gets to hot it will break and the oil will separate if this happens don't panic, take it off of the heat and slowly mix in a whole raw egg white and all and keep mixing, it will come together as it cools.

Don't worry about clarified butter or any crap like that it is more about being fancy then it is about function.

Once the sauce is ready break four eggs into the boiling water, three minutes will poach them nicely but what you are looking for is the egg to float half way from the bottom of the pot to the surface this indicates they are ready. Oh and by the way the vinegar we added to the water tightens the white of the egg and helps to keep it together.

While the eggs are poaching toast two buttered English muffins (that's four pieces total) on the grill.

Assembly, place two halves of toasted muffins toast side up on a plate cover each with Crawfish mix, removing eggs one at a time with a slotted spoon place one eggs each on seafood mix on muffin and then gently spoon Hollandaise sauce over egg, garnish with a pinch of paprika, repeat on second plate and serve with Mimosa or Bloody Mary or a nice spring ice tea.

Fred Style, for vegetarians replace the Canadian bacon and seafood with a nice big grilled slice of tomato the kind known as "Beef Eaters"...of which I never tire of pointing out to her. The rest remains the same.

10:00 BREAK

AMID MORNING SNACK IS a good idea as I said earlier it keeps the motor running and helps to burn the fuel in your body to keep fat from building up but let's not use this as an excuse to wolf down a pound of Twinkies. Here are a few ideas for snacks you can make ahead of time; of course a simple piece of fruit or some raw vegetables are always best. It was said that friends of my grandfather from whom my middle name proudly comes, (my first name as proudly from his wife my grandmother) would set their watches by his 10:00 apple. Those baby carrots we mentioned earlier come in handy here as well as a bunch of grapes or some cherries all of which provide the stuff that keeps you healthy and your energy up…You see if you fill your stomach with a lot of stuff then the body has to take energy from the rest of you to process all the stuff you put in your belly…it's just common sense really. So eat a lot but eat light. Bananas are a great snack food with or without the peanut butter, but this stuff can be boring so let's see what else we can come up with.

Trail Mix

Is always fun and can be good for you too, try to leave out the sweet stuff like marshmallows and chocolate chips and make it up at home or have fun with it on your 34, don't be afraid to improvise and do your own thing. Here is an outline of one idea.

Using your coffee cup for measuring take half a cup of shaved almonds and spread them out on a cookie sheet. Add a half cup of pecan pieces, then bake the nuts in your toaster oven at 350 degrees for about five minutes or until they get nice and brown. If you don't have a toaster oven or don't care for toasted nuts just skip this part. When the nuts are G.B.D. pull them out of the oven and set them somewhere safe to cool.

In a bowl like maybe a plastic bowl with a cover about 2 quarts in size found easily at the dollar stores, pour in a cup of dried cranberries, 1 cup of raisins (I like the white ones), 1 cup of dried cherries, half a cup of small pretzel sticks and a half cup of cashews, (preferably salt free or light salt). Add the nuts once cool and mix it all together. Store it in the covered bowl this does not require refrigeration.

This is both healthy and tasty as well as very easy and again it is an outline, create your own and don't be shy. Just remember what dad always says and keep it simple, you will be much happier in the end. You can find these ingredients and others in most stores and farmer markets, (very cool places to shop) also buy them in bulk at places such as United Grocers, Sam's, Costco, and such.

Cheese Puffs

This is another Fred recipe you can make in advance and she says they are awesome…actually she said people have called them food crack, so you have been warned.

Soften but not melted butter about a stick or quarter pound. You can soften it by letting it sit out for a while or microwave it for about 10 seconds at a time until it is soft enough to work with.

Add about a half cup of flour but be ready to add more.

Add about a cup of shredded extra sharp cheddar cheese and mix this all together with your hands, (remember wash them and or put on gloves) until you have something like Play Dough. Fred says she uses lots of cheese so add more of that first to get the dough effect and then flour if you need it, if it is too dry add more butter. Once you have play dough, roll it into little balls about half the size of a golf ball, line them up on a cookie sheet with about a finger tip between them and bake them at 350 degrees for 15-20 minutes. Longer for crispy cheese puffs, shorter for softer cheese puffs, Make up a bunch in advance to give you days of munchies.

Now Fred offers some options for different kinds of cheese puffs, you can add rice crispies to the mix to give you crunchy puffs, or add hot peppers chopped up to spice them up. Also feel free to change the cheese she says that pepper jack cheese work great too!

We are only here to give you the tools what you build is up to you.

Lazy Guacamole

Mole is an Aztec word which means, "to grind"…generally with a mortar and pestle, but we don't have time so this is my lazy way out.

Into your soup bowl dice 2 medium tomatoes, 1 small onion, and 2 jalapenos (less for mild taste more for hotter taste). This is Pico De Gallo, (the beak of the rooster, or phallus) which are the colors of the Mexican flag red for tomato, white for onion, and green for jalapenos and if anyone tells you different their wrong.

Now to this mix add two shots of lemon or lime juice or a mix of both. I like the lime best but it's up to you. Chop up a stalk or two of cilantro and remember as with oregano a little goes a long way too much cilantro will ruin the dish.

Mix this all together and set it off to the side, (the longer it sits the more the flavor improves)

Cut and seed two avocados by slicing the avocado from top to bottom and all the way around, then twisting it apart, Now holding the side with the seed in it gently chop the seed with your knife allowing the blade to stick in the seed. Turn knife and seed as if winding a clock and remove the seed, with your thumb on the back of the seed and against the blade of the knife pop the seed off the blade and into the trash. Place the four avocado halves on their skin with the cut half and seed hole facing up, fill the holes with your salsa mix and sprinkle on a little cayenne pepper and granulated garlic if you like and just eat them out of the skin with a spoon.

Equipment note;

Magic Bullets are the bomb and a biscuit! I love the little suckers and they are great for us guys who are only trying to feed ourselves because they are small. I do not include them in the equipment list because they are not cheap and there for a luxury item. Just the same Wal-Mart carries the full set for around $50.00 and if you can afford it they rock!

You can take all the stuff from above including the avocado scooped out of the skin and cut in chunks. Put all this in a Magic Bullet and puree it into guacamole which you can then enjoy with chips, crackers, or toast or whatever you choose.

Options

If you enjoy avocados but not so much the south of the border spicy stuff try filling the hole with a crab dip, or chicken salad, tuna salad or any such thing. To make these is easy, dice up a trinity (equal parts of celery, bell pepper, onion) dice up cooked or preferably smoked chicken hit it with a dash of sea salt, cayenne and granulated garlic, mix in enough mayonnaise to make it moist but not soupy and there you go chicken salad. It's the very same thing for crab, tuna (drain first if using canned) or shrimp salad just leave out the chicken and add a dash of dill weed or a splash or lemon juice…or both.

Finally

If you are not already drinking water see to it you do about a gallon a day more if you can, this is the stuff that oils your pipes and keeps everything running smooth and is about 86% of what we are so we need to keep it flowing if you can't carry that much Google foods that are high in water such as cucumbers which are full of the stuff as is pineapple, and lettuce, enough of that back to work.

LUNCH

I recommend a hot cup of soup and a sandwich or salad.

WRAPS

Warm 8-10 inch flour tortillas in your microwave for 10 seconds or so or in one of those cool clay tortilla things if you have one, (not worth getting one unless you eat a lot of tortillas)

Wrap wrapping 101

Place warm 10 inch tortilla on flat service or plate, in the lower center put about 4 tablespoons of your mix. Leave about an inch of empty tortilla on either end, fold the sides first then bring the bottom edge over your mix and roll upwards. Just before getting to the top bring the outer leading edges in this will "tuck" the wrap. This too is more art than science so don't sweat it if you screw up a few…I still do.

The following are my own creations that I use to feed vegetarians at sea, feel free to add meat of choice and cheese or remove what you don't like. The ingredients given can be sliced or diced and where it says grilled you can steam them in the microwave in a covered container with a few teaspoon of water and a way for the steam to escape, like a tooth pick hole in the plastic wrap cover. You can also leave them raw, or toast them with the toaster oven, just rub them with a little olive oil first for a better flavor.

1.) Cucumber Wrap

½ Cucumber, 1 Avocado, ½ Tomato, 3 leaves Romaine Lettuce, Teaspoon Chopped Cilantro, 2 Shots Lime Juice, (I usually make a salad of this and then just fill a wrap with it.)

2.) Garden Wrap

3 peeled slices of Cantaloupe, 3 leaves Romaine Lettuce, ¼ Red Onion, 4 Medium Mushrooms, ½ Shredded Carrot, Pinch of Dill Weed, 1 ½ Shots Rice Vinegar, (Same as above)

3.) Holiday Wrap

Cranberry Sauce, Grilled Sweet Potatoes, Yellow Squash, and Zucchini (This would work great with some leftover turkey and is good hot or cold, I like the squash raw but it's up to you.)

4.) Italian Vegetable Wrap

2 Roma Tomatoes, 3 leaves Romaine Lettuce, ¼ Red Onion, Small Handful Sundried Tomatoes, ½ Zucchini, Italian Dressing to taste

5.) Margarita Wrap

6 Fresh Basil Leaves or tablespoon dry, 3 Roma Tomatoes, Mozzarella to taste, 3 Romaine Lettuce Leaves, 2 Shots Lime Juice

6.) Vegetable Dips/French Dips/Philly's

Grilled (or toasted) Hoagie Rolls, Grilled Tomatoes, Red Onion, Mushroom, Swiss cheese, and Vegetable stock for dipping, or remove vegetables and add roast beef in beef broth for French Dips, Steam or sauté some bell pepper with some onion lay this on moist roast beef on the toasted bun cover with provolone cheese and microwave until melted this is a Philly in the field. There are all kinds of stocks and broths out there just watch that sodium level stocks are the worst! Pay attention to Goya brand stocks, they still have the salt but these people are serious about what they do and are in my opinion doing cutting edge things with simple stocks…not to mention they have a bunch of powdered stocks which are great for what we are trying to do. Tomato soup is also a good dip…and speaking of which.

SOUPS

Needless to say scores of plumes have been put to ink over a simple cup of soup. Europeans swear by soup with lunch and as I have found so does most of the working world and why not? The heat from a cup of soup alone is soothing and comforting and it does not matter if it's 100 degrees outside soup is just a darn good way to do lunch, (I do not include cold soups in here because I don't understand them and don't want to…I mean cucumber soup…to me it's a dip.)

Bering Sea Tomato Soup

Pour some V8 juice in a soup bowl and microwave it until it's hot and if you must add a shot of milk to it.

Hay, I have never read in any cook book anywhere that this stuff has to be complicated to be good.

Cheese sandwich cheat, toast two slices of bread, put a couple of slices of cheese in between and microwave it until cheese melts about 10 second or so.

B.L.T. cheat, microwave four strips of bacon, toast two slices of bread combine with sliced tomato and lettuce with a bit of mayo. (Your cost about 50 cents, what do you pay for one at the truck stop?)

B.L.A.T., same as above but add a slice of avocado, about 54 cents and very California.

Egg Drop Soup

You need pretty hot water for this so boil some on a burner in a pot or if you must boil a half bowl of water in the microwave and using chicken bouillon cubes or stock, or if you are a vegetarian then vegetable bullion or stock. Make a broth, in a separate bowl or coffee cup break two eggs and with your fork break the yolks and kind of mix them up a bit but leave them kind of loose. With the stock as hot as you safely can make it swirl the stock in circles as you slowly pour the eggs into it. Remove the soup from the heat if it is still on the heat and let it rest a few minutes in the mean time chop up a tablespoon of green onion and sprinkle them on the soup…and ladies and gentlemen that is all there is to egg drop soup.

Options

I have always loved Egg Drop soup but find it boring so to mine I add diced tofu, a little brown miso (soybean paste), and some crumbled up Nori (that's the black seaweed they wrap sushi in). Also a dash of any Oriental pepper or pepper mix is nice like Nanami Togarashi; rice seasoning also has most of the stuff I use already in it. The beauty of such a simple soup is that you can leave it simple or go crazy with it…in the end…you guessed it, it's all up to you.

Cream of Mushroom Soup

Yup! You can get this by the can anywhere, you can also get tons of soups by the can and fill your cab with them…but that is not why we are here and I can do it cheaper, healthier and damn near just as fast.

Get your soup bowl, slice in about 6 nice mushrooms, 2 or 3 shots of those diced onions I hear you got laying around and a tablespoon of butter, (by the way if you don't have a tablespoon it's 3 teaspoons…just so you know)

Cover the bowl in plastic, poke a hole in the middle with a toothpick and microwave it for 3-5 minutes or until you smell onion and mushrooms cooking. Pull it out and yes it will be hot…duh, add a few teaspoons of flour to make that wet paste we call roux, slowly pour milk in as you mix it into the roux until you get something sort of smooth, (it will probably not be very smooth). Back in the microwave for about another 5 minutes stirring it every few minutes…add more milk if it's to thick, cook it longer if to thin salt and pepper to taste and there it is mushroom soup homemade in more or less the same time it takes to nuke a can.

Chicken Noodle Soup

Why does chicken noodle soup help when you have a cold? Because of the high levels of Bata keratins in it which comes from the carrots and parsley and of which you're not really going to find in a can, are you?

If you can put this together in your crock pot in the morning it is best but understanding that this is not an easy thing to do, I give you this stove top version you can do in the microwave as well. The only thing that is important here is to get fresh carrots and parsley if possible.

Get the ole pot of water a boiling on the stove top, you can use raw or cooked chicken for this not much difference except the raw may give you a bit more flavor. In a perfect world I like to make mine with left over smoked chicken...but as you get to know me you'll see I smoke everything when I can...even pecan cookies on pecan chips...yum...

O.K. then into the pot goes diced chicken again raw or cooked, assuming you have one of those Paula Dean pots we talked about so long ago I'm thinking about half your coffee cup full of diced chicken followed by the same amount of diced carrots, yellow onion, and celery. This is a lot of vegetables but this is a healthy soup with a chicken flavor. About two bouillon cubes of the chicken variety or a teaspoon of stock/base, pinch of basil, oregano, and thyme, small pinch of sea salt and cayenne pepper, (here is a good example of cayenne as a flavor enhancer, you should not actually taste it in this dish but should get a full body warm and fuzzy feeling from it while eating this soup.). Allow all this to boil until the carrots are nice and soft adding more water if you need it to keep it soupy. Now this part is just for you, pasta on the road can be a pain and left over pasta often turns mushy, so into the pot you now stir Orzo pasta which is pasta that looks like large rice and cooks in about 9 minutes or less. Remember pasta absorbs water and swells so a little goes a long way I would put about 2-3 tablespoons of Orzo into your soup stirring it often. While the orzo is cooking chop up a big tablespoon of fresh parsley and once the pasta is soft stir in the parsley remove it from the heat and lunch is served. The whole process should not take more than about twenty minutes with a bit of practice and as you cook more you will get to know what you use the most and keep these thing prepared, (or "prepped") and ready…like our sandwich bag of diced onions.

Salads

The wraps above are salads in a wrap…so just leave off the wrap. I am not going to insult your intelligence or waste your time by giving you recipes for making salads. What I will say is that if you do eat salads often then you are already serious about being healthy so here are a few things to note. Dark greens have more good things in them, lighter greens are mostly water and Ice Berg lettuce has almost no nutritional value but is high in water. Mushrooms as well have very little nutritional value but there is a school of thought that argues that point rather well so I will stay on the middle of that fence and since I like the flavor of mushrooms and they make me happy I will continue to eat them. If you are making a meal of your salad then by all means Cobb on out, top that puppy with cheese, eggs, ham, whatever suits you, but if the salad is a side try not to eat twice…if you know what I mean. Also going back to our little oatmeal talk, if you need to cover your salad in some creamy fatty dressing just to choke it down, then just stop you are only fooling yourself.

Healthy tip; Alfalfa is known to help with joint pain and swelling and I know truckers hurt and creak all the time. So use alfalfa sprouts in your salads, found with the fresh herbs in most stores or drink alfalfa tea, this you might have to get at a health food store and to me it tastes dusty.

Finally, the French believe in eating their salad after the meal so the roughage can better assist with digestion…and so do I.

1500 HOURS AND BREAK TIME

This is where I usually serve sushi and such things focusing on light proteins to help replace what you've used and get you to the end of the day. Also fruit like oranges, grapefruit and such are good along with some cheeses…let's see what we can come up with. The Chief and I are famous for standing around the kitchen in the afternoon with a bunch of stuff spread across the counter like cheese and ham, or some smoked salmon, sardines, smoked oysters or dry fish, salami, olives, carrot sticks, celery sticks (fill these with peanut butter or cream cheese) and whatever else we can find. We just lay it all out and have our standing afternoon snack or as the Chief would call it our "Bachelor Buffett".

Oh, Cool Side note; Chewing on celery sticks cleans and scrubs the teeth, if you don't have time to brush between meals just chew on a celery stalk or two.

Hummus

Go ahead roll your eyes and say all those nasty things we all say about food that's good for us it's just a left over gut reaction from childhood when Momma wanted us to eat our vegetables. Now think about it, hummus comes from a part of the world where in the day, the day meant survival. It is often considered a delicacy because the ingredients were so hard to come by and were good for you…now a days when something is a delicacy it generally means that it's about as good for you as crack, but there was a time when this was not so and hummus comes from that time… An example of what I mean about things we giggle about being delicacies for others, I was on a processor in the Bering Sea with 220 people 80% were kids from many of the countries of Africa. One day this young man from Ethiopia came to me and in a very nervous voice asked if he could have some Paprika, well I was busy and did not give it much thought I just grabbed the jug of paprika which was about 3 pounds worth and handed it to him. The man was frozen in place shaking like a leaf and staring at this jug of paprika, there were several of his countrymen that just stopped in place as well. It took some time for me to sort it all out but apparently there is a dish in his country that is made of warm olive oil mixed with paprika and you dip bread into it, this is to them a delicacy and paprika is so rare there that to have this dish is their equivalent of fine caviar. The young man from Africa was standing there holding more paprika then anyone in his country had ever seen in their entire lives, it was as he told me later like handing me a bag of diamonds and saying "Help yourself". So what is fu-fu to you may be a god send to your neighbor…the world is shrinking and food is the tell tale. For those of us with a little age can you remember a time when the word "Sushi" was not even known? Now you can buy it at Wal-Mart…think about it.

So! Here we go; hummus is a dip or spread usually served with pita bread which is great for you because a little goes a long way. Buy a small package of pita bread, lay a slice down on your cutting board and cut it into pie pieces whatever size turns you on.

This is another good one for the magic bullet but if you don't have one that's o.k. in your soup bowl pour one can of drained Chick Peas or Garbanzo Beans, what the difference…the spelling. Drizzle in a good shot of olive oil, a shot of sesame oil, a shot of lemon juice, a good sprinkling of granulated garlic, and a dash of cayenne pepper along with a pinch of sea salt if you must. Mush it all together with your fork or spoon or whatever works for you until you have a dip like substance adjust the flavors to your liking remembering that the lemon juice will bring the flavors out more while the cayenne enhances them and can become over powering as will the garlic so play with it, if you are just not getting the kick you want that is the time to add a bit more sea salt…and now time for a cheesy poem;

"None of this stuff is chiseled in stone, just keep tweaking it and make it your own."

Yup, not quitting the day job any time soon…

Candied Pecans

Not a healthy snack but hay, all work and no play…

Ridiculously easy, start your little pot of water boiling and once it is throw in two handfuls of pecan halves or walnut halves or a mix of both. Let them boil; (blanch) for about a minute or two. Drain off the water and pour the nuts into your soup bowl, and just like cereal dump 2 spoonfuls of powdered sugar on top as well as half a teaspoon of cinnamon and half a teaspoon of nutmeg and if you have it a half teaspoon of ground cloves. Mix this all together coating the nuts as best you can. Now spread them out on a well greased baking sheet, (pan spray from the dollar store) and bake them in your toaster oven on 350 for about 10-15 minutes or until they get G.B.D. Set them aside to cool somewhere safe and once cool, (if you haven't eaten them already) with your nylon spatula scrape them off the sheet pan and store them in a sandwich bag…Oh I also suggest you cover the baking sheet with tin foil it saves on clean up these things can get a bit sticky while hot.

Shrimp Cocktail

This is always popular in the afternoon, buy whatever raw shrimp you like. Shrimp and many other things are sold by average weight counts so if you see a bag of shrimp that says 26-30, what that means is there are about 26-30 shrimp in a pound in that bag. We as cooks use this to calculate pricing where as you can use this to balance your diet knowing that if you eat 30 of these shrimp you just ate a pound of shrimp which is easily twice what you should be eating, (really 4 times but who is going to eat just 7 shrimp?).

Start your water boiling again, or fill your soup bowl with as many shrimp as you want and yes straight from the freezer is fine, and cover them with water. I buy the ones that are peeled but if you don't mind peeling those are cheaper because no one was paid to peel them. Microwave your bowl of shrimp and water until the water starts to boil and then leave it alone to cool, as with the boiling water on your burner if you have one once it is boiling put in the frozen shrimp bring it back to a boil and then turn off the heat and let it cool. Now the entire culinary community will tell you that I am nuts and that you need to boil your seafood until it is done…Well, have you ever had shrimp that is the texture of rubber? Now you know why, steep your fresh seafood like you steep a cup of tea…ops, truck drivers…well just trust me and let the shrimp sit in the hot water while it cools and then make sure they are nice and pink into the refrigerator to cool. Also when placing hot stuff in the refrigerator to cool it is important to note that you should not cover anything completely as this slows down the cooling and allows bacteria to grow and if you ever put hot beans in the refrigerator covered only to come back the next day and find them sour this is the reason, so cover yes but allow air to escape until cool.

Cocktail Sauce

Fill your coffee cup about a quarter way with ketchup, (Heinz makes this very cool 10 ounce pouch of ketchup that stores very well for your needs) add one teaspoon of horseradish more if you like it hot less if you don't and about as much lemon juice and mix it all together and that is cocktail sauce.

Tartar Sauce

A quarter cup of mayonnaise, (several companies now make shelf stable mayonnaise in squeeze bottles, look on the label and buy the ones that say "does not need refrigeration") two teaspoons of sweet pickle relish and a teaspoon or two of lemon juice then just mix it up. I add a pinch of cayenne to mine just to jazz it up a bit.

Bean Dips

I add this here for two reasons one it is a great way to use leftover beans, and we will have left over beans, also it is a high in protein snack if you need a boost for an afternoon tying down tarps or some such thing.

Using any leftover bean that is completely cooked half fill your soup bowl, or magic bullet add a quarter coffee cup of the Pico de Gallo from our Lazy Guacamole recipe add a handful of your favorite shredded cheese or if you have a block or slices just chop up some cheese than mix it all together and microwave it until it's hot and melted stirring it a few times along the way.

Feel free to add other things as well such as sliced jalapenos or mix the beans and other herbs or spices. The only thing I will point out here is that beans are also carbohydrates which if not used by your body will turn to fat so try not to use to many crackers, chips, or breads with this dip. A good idea is taken from south of the border where tortillas are used for such things. Simply spread you bean dip on a little tortilla and roll it up like a cigar and down the road you go.

I conclude this snack time by pointing out as I have before that all I am doing here is giving you the tools to do your own thing. I am a bit of an outcast among my culinary piers because I think differently and speak my mind, one of the things that really ticks them off is that as far as I am concerned any left armed monkey can cook…what we do is improvise, we make magic out of mud. My own mother can make dirt taste good but in her case it's because of all the kitchen love she adds… and maybe in our case too.

DINNER TIME

The Crock Pot is My Friend

This section is all crock pot dinner recipes, two things to say about the crock pot. First load it in the morning as it needs to slow cook all day, dinner is ready when you can't take the smell anymore, and the Chief and I recommend you use Reynolds Slow Cooker Liners these can be found in any Wal-Mart where the paper plates are down by the cold wall as the Chief would call it…He is amazed that the entire wall is one massive cooler, and I am amused. O.k. that's three things…anyway, these crock pot liners are a great way to cut down on clean up, you can just put all the ingredients into the bag and if you want freeze it and then take the frozen bag of stuff stick it in the crock pot while your morning biscuit are baking and down the road you go.

A note to Reynolds; The only disadvantage to these great liners is that they only come in one size that I am aware of which is 3-6.5 quart pots and they are oval. I understand that they have made a universal product and I applaud them but once you see these things you will understand that they are huge, maybe they could make a smaller version. Just the same we are in the survival game and this is a great way to take a disadvantage and turn it into an advantage. For one thing these bags are so big that if you put the bag in your crock pot and then pull the extra bag up like a chimney and place the lid on the crock pot but inside the bag leaving the bag sticking up like a chimney this will keep any over flows in the bag and off the upholstery. Also for tougher meats, like the cheap cuts of beef you and I general can only afford you can fold the bag in on itself and then place the lid on top of the bag sealing the food inside the bag and allowing it to steam the meat a bit more tender. Just the same some tough meat just stays that way so this is a patch and not a cure.

Chili by the Chief

1 pound of ground meat (beef or turkey)

1 teaspoon of garlic

1 teaspoon onion powder

2 teaspoons chili powder

½ teaspoon salt

½ teaspoon pepper

½ teaspoon ground mustard

½ white onion diced

½ of a bell pepper diced

1 small can of tomato sauce

1 small can of tomato paste

For medium heat 1 small can of diced green chilies

For hot heat 1 small can of diced jalapenos

1 can of kidney beans or black beans

It is better to brown the meat before adding it to the crock pot but it is not necessary, all this does is remove some of the fat which may make your chili greasy but we can get around that.

Add everything to your crock pot cover and cook on low 4-6 hours cut time roughly in half if you set the crock pot on high. Stir your chili as often as your time allows, if you do not have time to stir it don't panic. Just expect your ground meat to be sort of lumped up, it will break up again when you stir it before serving it.

Slurry is my favorite cheat, if your cooked chili is greasy put about two big spoonfuls of corn starch in your coffee cup and then add about a quarter of the cup of cold water, stir this up real good, this is the slurry. Now add this to the chili and stir very well, this will bind with the grease and make gravy. Add more if needed but careful too much will make your chili taste starchy.

Taco Soup by our Gal Sal

My niece Sally who is one of the Chief's tribe is a force unto herself and if ever there was a contest for ruler of the universe my vote is for her. Gal Sal says her recipe was designed to be for vegetarians but all you need is to add meat like the Chiefs chili if you want and if it's greasy don't forget the slurry recipe in the Chief's chili.

> 2 cans of any bean you like Sally recommends mixing one can of kidney beans with one can of black beans (Apple don't fall far from the tree ay Chief)
>
> 1 can of cream corn
>
> 1 can of stewed tomatoes with green chilies
>
> 1 packet taco seasoning
>
> Tortilla chips or Frito's

Stir together first four ingredients and heat in the crock pot if using raw ground meat cook for several hours or until the smell makes you park your rig.

If greasy tighten with slurry (see the Chief's Chili)

Top your bowl full of taco soup with chips or Frito's and any other taco topping that turns you on like sour cream, or shredded cheese, black olives, etc…

Chicken Alfredo Ala Eric

Eric is one of the guys that runs with the Chief and has been an active part of our test kitchens from the beginning and I apologize that I have not said more about him, but I think this recipe speaks volumes. This is the essence of what was meant when Dad said "Keep it simple stupid" (K.I.S.S.). Originally Eric would take this dish and in the last two hours turn the pot up to high and add the pasta, unfortunately this would often cause the pasta to lump up, also left over dishes with pasta in them often turn to paste by the next day. So now Eric adds the pasta when he parks for the night and stirs it while he is doing his log book and such things. So with all due respect to Eric and the addition he has made to our adventure I now add the cooks touch. Orzo pasta which is very common is pasta that looks like large pieces of rice and will cook in about 9 minutes whereas most pasta takes 20 minutes or more, in addition egg noodles are also very fast cooking about 9 minutes. So I would suggest that with this dish remove what you want to save for a left over if anything and then add either of these pastas Orzo for small noodles and egg noodles for large noodles and only enough for the meal. If room allows and you eat a lot of pasta you can make plain pasta up during your 34, cool it add a little oil and bag it in the fridge for use during the week so then it only needs to get hot. Honestly though the dry stuff stores better so why bother unless as I said you eat a lot of pasta.

Take a couple of good sized chicken breasts or chicken tenders of equal amount and cut them into chunks.

Cover this in the crock pot with a large jar of Alfredo sauce (Eric says he also uses two jars of the regular size)

Cover and heat on low, when you reach your night stop add a

good handful of either pastas mentioned above and stir every few minutes until the pasta is tender. Also the pasta will suck up any juice from the chicken.

The Chief says this one was cooked between Spokane, Washington and Snowville, Utah to give you gear jammers an idea of cook time.

Simple, filling, and elegant…thanks Eric!

I would add a piece of garlic bread, simply cut open a bun or take a piece of bread or two get them damp with olive oil sprinkle granulated garlic and dry basil on the bread and toast it in the toaster oven. This is traditional Garlic bread.

Sauce Cheat; Alfredo sauce is milk or cream with salt, pepper, and nutmeg in it as well as melted parmesan cheese. To save some money just follow Eric's recipe except instead of Alfredo by the jar cover the chicken with milk add a little sea salt and cayenne, nutmeg if you have it, if not no big deal. Cook just like Eric says and then when you park add the pasta and when it's tender, thicken up the sauce with parmesan cheese start with 1 cup of cheese and go from there. The pasta supplies the starch and the cheese and chicken the protein to make this thicken up nicely. Also buy the cheap parmesan in the can because they use a chemical to keep it from caking which actually helps your sauce to become creamy.

Ribs Rubbed Right

Country pork ribs are a boneless cut and will easily fit in your crock pot, if your pot is oval bone in ribs might work.

Rub

About a ¼ inch of olive oil on the bottom of your soup bowl

1 teaspoon cinnamon

½ teaspoon nutmeg

½ teaspoon sea salt

½ teaspoon paprika

½ teaspoon cayenne pepper or chipotle pepper

Mix this all together and rub generously on about a pound of country pork ribs. Place ribs in crock pot as well as about half of an onion sliced. If using a crock pot liner fold the liner in on itself and cover allowing the ribs to steam themselves. Cook on low for 4-6 hours or again until the smell is strong, if there is a great deal of juice try to pour some off. If juice is low just add a few spoons of flour and stir until you have a paste then cover with your favorite B.B.Q. Sauce cover until sauce is hot about ten minutes or so and there you go.

B.B.Q. Chicken

Same as above using two legs or the equivalent amount of chicken

Recommended sides

Baked potatoes

Fred says that sweet potatoes and baked potatoes are great in the micro wave and they are, wash the dirt off them and microwave until they are soft. Time will vary from microwave to microwave but 10 minutes per potato is a good place to start.

Cob Corn

One of my favorites from Fred, she says to take an ear of corn husk and all and microwave it for about 4 minutes per ear. Then cut the back off and pull the ear of corn from the husk leaving silk and all behind. I mean come on guys (and gals) We just showed you how to make your own B.B.Q. with baked potato and cob corn on the road in your rig for about a ¼ of what you would pay for it at a nice B.B.Q. hut and that's if you could find one... almost forgot the tea.

Sun Tea

Can't claim to have lived in the Carolinas and not be able to make sweet sun tea, in a clear quart jar add ¼ cup of sugar, fill half way with water close and shake to mix sugar. Open and add 4 teabags of cup size and fill remainder of jar with water, close lid and place in the sun until dark enough probably several hours.

Tuna Tetrazzini

Into the crock pot goes;

2 regular or one big can of tuna, drained

½ of an onion diced

2 teaspoons butter

1 fat fist full of sliced mushrooms

2 stalks of chopped parsley or a teaspoon of dry

1 teaspoon lemon juice

½ teaspoon paprika

Cover everything with milk plus a fingers breath…about 1 inch

Cook on low for 4-6 hours

When hot and bubbly add a small handful of egg noodles and stir often until soft, then thicken the sauce with parmesan start with 1 cup and go from there.

JAG Rice from Cape Verde

A group of islands off the coast of Western Africa where the people are friendly and the rum is as warm as the sun...I do miss it so...

Into the pot we go with;

1 small onion diced

2 shots of olive oil

1 cup of cooked beans (you can use dry beans but might have to add more water later in the cooking and it will take a little longer to cook)

1 cup of water

½ cup rice

A pinch of sea salt

A dash of paprika

About a half pound of sliced sausage (I like Linguicia any kind is good)

Cover and cook on low until rice is cooked and beans are soft about 4-6 hours

Mom's Meatloaf

What, you didn't think I could do this without getting D.O.M. (dear ole Mom) involved?

>   1 pound ground meat of choice (half and half of beef and pork is nice)

>   A couple of shots of diced onion, celery, and bell pepper

>   3 raw eggs

>   1 cup of Italian bread crumbs

>   ¼ flour (only here to keep grease level low if baking in an oven omit the flour)

>   A dash of Worcestershire sauce

>   A little salt and pepper

Mix this all together until everything is nice and even, you may actually be able to put it into the liner and use the bag to mix it, if not maybe mix it in the crock pot itself. Generally I mix this with my hands because it's pretty tough stuff, just remember to wash and, or use the gloves

Pack this into the crock pot making a nice solid piece in the bottom, cover and cook on low 4-6 hours. There may be a bit of grease in the pot when it's done pour this off if possible then cover the top of the meat loaf with ketchup and continue to cook for another 10 minutes or until the ketchup is hot and a little glazed over.

Meatball Cheat; Mom's meatloaf is also the same basic recipe for meatballs you can leave it as is or jazz it up with some parmesan or other kind of cheese mixed in or maybe some hot peppers. In any case just take the mix from above and role it into little meatballs a little smaller then a golf ball. It is best to bake these at least part way to seal them so they won't fall apart in the sauce but if you can't bake them microwave them for a little bit…just enough so you see a little juice bubbling out about 5-8 minutes. If you are cooking with these right away then into the sauce they go if not you can freeze them of cool them in the fridge for later.

The Chief's Meatloaf

Yes there are many different kinds and that is my point. The Chief says this works well, there is grease around it when it's done he said he ran it off with a slotted spoon. The only negative thing is he said it was a little bland and wanted to know what I would suggest…Well brother I would suggest that you go to the last recipe and start listening to your mommy, but in absence of that let's see what we can do. First his recipe and then we tweak it a bit.

2 pound of ground beef

2 cups of oatmeal

2 eggs

½ of an onion diced

A good healthy shake of granulated garlic

1 can of stewed tomatoes 15 ounce, drained

Mix together well, pack down into the crock pot and cook for 4-6 hours on low.

O.k. that's it…anything wrong with it, nope not a darn thing just the same two things come to mind. As I recall D.O.M. used the Italian bread crumbs as her cheat because they had all the herbs and stuff already in them. The Chief used oatmeal because then he did not have to buy a special ingredient as he already had oatmeal for other stuff, good improvise. Also he did not have ketchup on hand so he left it out…o.k. but in this case the ketchup helps keep it moist and gives it a kick in the end. Can you leave it off, sure you can but balance must be maintained… so, what would I do?

Add ¼ cup of beef broth to give more flavor (and it has the salt as well)

A dash of Worcestershire is an all around one, it covers all kinds of ingredient if you carry this you can eliminate many others

And some kind of pepper, white, black, red you know I like the red but you know you can even use those pizza peppers... just something to jazz it up a bit.

You do not have to sauce it but even the best of meat loaf tastes better with something on it but that is only my opinion and I'm not eating this you are. So if you want to top it but don't have ketchup you can use a can of mushroom soup, tomato soup, thicken some V-8 with a slurry and use that…how about B.B.Q. sauce or maybe some Teriyaki…it simply does not matter what you use as long as it makes you happy. I had a wonderful Captain once, Captain Pat one of my favorites and Captain Pat loved pepperoni and smoked oyster pizzas…I never could get my tongue wrapped around them but the man loved them so I made them and loved doing it for him.

Authors Note;

The Chief and I come from a simpler time, a harder and harsher time but none the less simpler and in many ways I think we would like to go back there…maybe without so much of the harder and harsher. This I feel is a great deal of what I am trying to present to you, I was just sitting here going through my notes and my morning coffee when I picked up a copy of "the Best of Backwoodsman" a paperback book of sorts with all kinds of survival stuff in it. Looking at the recipes in the back and I am sure some of these date back a long time I was tickled at how simple and basic things were and in many ways should still be like beer bread made with three ingredients, and stews of diced bacon and beef jerky. If you enjoy a step back in time as well as a little common sense knowledge pick up some of these they're small and easy to read not sure where to find them but Google knows. Two other good books for helping your health in an old world less politically correct sort of way would be "Vermont Folk Medicine" and "Back to Eden"…sorry I don't remember the authors as I have once again loaned out my copies and they have gone missing.

Edith Smith's Drunken Chicken

Can't really make this one on the road but I would be remiss if I did not pay tribute to one of the sweetest most wonderful ladies to have blessed this old rock, may she rest in peace.

Fill your crock pot about ¾ full of raw chicken

Add 1 can of diced tomatoes with green chilies

Add one can of beer, (note use cheap beer get cheap flavor)

Cover and cook on low 4-6 hours, goes good with biscuits… but what doesn't

Swedish Meatballs

Using the meatball recipe from Mom's meatloaf, a dozen or so meatballs in your crock pot

Add 1 small onion sliced

Add a good handful of sliced mushrooms

Add one can of mushroom soup

Add one cup of water

Cover and cook on low 4-6 hours or until bubbly

You can add egg noodles or just eat it like this

If you don't have mushroom soups just add a few teaspoons of butter along with enough milk to cover everything and then just tighten it up with slurry when done.

Teriyaki Meatballs

Teriyaki sauce is simply soy sauce pineapple juice and brown sugar, the easy way to do this is with bottled sauce but if you want the cheap way out here we go.

1 dozen meatballs into the crock pot

½ of a small onion sliced

½ of a bell pepper sliced

½ cup of soy sauce

1 cup of pineapple juice (I prefer orange juice and apple works well too)

¼ cup brown sugar

If available add a half can of drained chunked pineapple

Cover and cook on low for about 4 hours stirring whenever you can, this is done when it is thick and bubbly

Serve over rice, you can mix raw rice into this about an hour before it's done but it will not look pretty as the rice will absorb the color, but on the road who cares. Also if you don't have the means to cook rice then I recommend instant rice which of course coats a bit more but it works great.

Pork and Beans

Into the crock pot goes

1 Ham Hock

1 cup of dry pinto beans (rinse these off first and make sure there no stones in them)

1 small onion diced

1 jalapeno pepper seeded and diced (can use green chilies for less heat or leave out altogether)

3 cups of water

Cover and cook all day or until beans are soft

This and That; You might have noticed that I don't use a great deal of stocks or bases, this is because the salt content of these things are simply too high. Feel free to add a little to give more flavor and I bring this up now because of this recipe with a little ham stock it will give it a great flavor but just a little or it will be way to salty to eat…you see the ham hock already has plenty of salt usually about 60%. Also this is the first recipe in the book to call for dry beans, I wanted you to feel comfortable cooking so prior to this we did not get into the dry beans but there really is nothing to them, again the culinary gurus would cringe but there really is no need to soak a bean especially in the crock pot which slow cooks all day. In a stove top pot get the beans to a boil lower the heat to a simmer for an hour and then get them boiling again until tender. Generally about six times the water to beans but that's an average I use about half of that and add water as the beans soak it up, cook only what you need with beans as they do not store well when cooked and if they smell even a little funny get rid of them.

A Nice Touch

My personal favorite (o.k. one of them) is to take the cornbread recipe from the baking section of this book and about an hour before dinner I will make the batter and pour it on top of the pork and beans, cover the pot and let the cornbread bake on top like a dumpling, when it feels dense to the touch it's done.

Options

Many cultures such as the Cajuns, Creole, and Gullah use sausage instead of many ingredients to flavor their dishes and then enhance these flavors by balancing out the cayenne pepper with things like lemon juice.

A nice twist to the pork and beans would be to replace the ham hock with your favorite sausage or leave it in and add sausage as well. If you do this with kidney beans and pour it over rice you have red beans and rice.

Quinn Shrimp

If it fits take an ear of corn cut it in half and put it into your crock pot, if not add about a cup of frozen corn

1 big fat handful of raw shrimp

½ pound of sliced sausage, something with a smoky flavor is nice

1 small potato cut into chunks

1 small jalapeno whole do not cut just put it into the pot

A little seafood stock or a teaspoon of butter with a pinch of sea salt

Splash of lemon juice

Pinch of cayenne pepper

Enough water to just cover everything

Cover and cook on low 4 hours or until the shrimp are pink

Goes nicely with cornbread

Chicken Gumbo

"Pictsweet" brand frozen vegetables has a gumbo vegetable mix that is awesome and I highly recommend it, just the same here is your basic gumbo New Orleans style, if you want Lake Charles style just leave out the okra.

In the pot

> 1 small chicken breast large dice

> A good handful of diced sausage Italian is nice in this Andoullie is best

> ½ cup of trinity (diced celery, bell pepper, and onion)

> 1 cup of frozen okra

> ½ cup of frozen corn (optional)

> 1 teaspoon of chicken stock

> A pinch of cayenne pepper

> Add enough water to just cover everything

Cover and cook on low 4-6 hours or until the chicken is done

In your soup bowl melt about 4 spoons of butter and then mix into it about 4 spoons of flour to make a paste or mud like roux, add the roux to the gumbo stirring it in well and allow to cook for about 10 minutes more or until nice and thick.

Pour over rice and enjoy, also nice with a glass of sun tea

Filet in the "Gumbo Filet" is nothing more than ground sassafras and if you don't have it I would not lose any sleep over it.

Beef Stew

By now something like beef stew should be a no brainer for you but I put it here for a very good reason, I do not know the exact science behind it but when slow cooking beef the water often draws the water out of the beef causing it to be tough and stringy, you can fix this by boiling the dog snot out of it but in a crock pot we don't have time for something like that which could literally take days. The Chief and I have tried several different tricks but they always end up changing the recipe more than I care to...so this is my cheat.

Using a small beef roast that will fit in your crock pot place the entire roast in the pot without cutting it up, cover and surround the roast with your favorite vegetables below is a guide line to the basics.

A handful of baby carrots

A small hand full of celery and diced onion

1 nice sized potato diced

A little chopped or dry parsley, the same with rosemary, and thyme, or basil (Italian seasoning is a good cheat)

Enough water to cover everything

Cover and cook on low 6-8 hours, what we really want is for the roast to start to fall apart not radically so but enough to start pulling off pieces. At this point if you can tear up the roast in the pot do so but it is probably too hot so pull it out and set it on you cutting board to cool a little while it's cooling melt 4 spoons of butter in the soup bowl in the microwave mix into the butter 4 spoons of flour and then mix this into the juice and vegetables in the pot stirring it in well and then cut up the roast and replace it into the stew.

It should be noted that you can also cook a roast of any kind beef, pork, Cornish hen whatever fits in the pot just put it in the liner or spray pan spay in the crock pot and a little salt pepper and what have you gets you a nice roast at day end.

See the baking section for a nice bread to use with the stew for dipping

Left over's

We conclude our crock pot section with two good examples of the use of leftovers.

American Sheppard's Pie

I say American because the original is a bit different and made with lamb, I hail from the Buffalo, New York area many years ago and I know the right way to make Buffalo Chicken Wings and it angers me to tears the way everybody sells Buffalo wings that are not even close to the real thing. Changing the recipe is fine; it's great but the name needs to change too.

Using leftover meat of any kind such as hamburgers, or cut up steak, or roast

Fill the bottom of you crock pot about 1/3 of the way

On top of the meat make a layer of frozen mixed vegetables

Make a broth of similar flavor such as beef broth to go with the beef, or chicken broth to go with chicken (ever wonder why everything tastes like chicken? Because Chef's put chicken stock in everything...even vegetarian dishes...ugg.) Enough to cover the meat and vegetables about 3 cups

After you have covered the meat and vegetables with stock fill the rest of the pot with mashed potatoes packing them down like a potato cover, you can use leftover baked potatoes that you mash with a little milk to soften them up or use instant potatoes the one from Idaho brand are great and real and don't cost much.

Sprinkle some cheese of choice on top of the potatoes if you like cheddar is generally used Cook covered for 4 hours or until the stock is starting to bubble up the sides of the potatoes

Scalloped Potatoes

Using leftover baked potatoes and any sort of pork, ham preferred

Slice about 3 potatoes into as thin a slice as you can safely cut

Slice or dice about 2 handfuls of ham or pork

Make a layer of sliced potatoes across the bottom of the crock pot

Then a layer of pork or ham

Sprinkle on a layer of parmesan cheese

Repeat this layering until the crock pot is about ¾ of the way full

Pour in enough milk to just cover everything and then one last layer of cheese

Cover and cook for 4-6 hours or until thick and bubbly

Option I left out the onion because I seem to have it in everything but a sliced onion in here is nice

TOASTER OVENS AND CHARCOAL GRILLS

WHAT YOU CAN DO with one you can do with the other, I hesitate here because we are not really sure how many of you actually have toaster ovens or grills. Just the same some do and that's enough.

If grilling during your 34 at a truck stop please make sure you can, safety first always and please be respectful. The Chief tells me of places where the outside grill has been banned in certain truck stops because of the wild party's thrown around them. Show respect first then expect it in return.

Call the manager of the truck stop you are planning on going to in order to see if grills are allowed, ask if a burn ban is in place or not. Your National Truck Stop Directory will have numbers and information to help as well as certain G.P.S. systems.

Kalbi Ribs (Korean Barbeque)

Please note these need to marinate for at least a day, so mix this in a Tupper ware container from the dollar store if you are on the road and let it sit in the refrigerator over night and through the next day. I am leaving a few things out as they are specialty items and not all that important but for those of you who want to add to the following 3 star anise, a small handful of lemon grass, as well as fresh ginger and garlic.

For the road though, in a 2 quart or so container with a tight fitting lid put about two pounds of beef short ribs, the kind that are cut thin are best but as long as they are beef, meaty, and fit in your container who cares.

Add to this

> 1 cups of soy sauce
>
> ¼ cup of sesame oil
>
> Two teaspoons brown sugar
>
> 1 teaspoon granulated garlic
>
> 1 teaspoon ginger powder
>
> 1 teaspoon red pepper flakes or ½ a teaspoon cayenne pepper

Mix this altogether coating the beef well, add just enough water to make sure everything is covered well, secure the lid and place in refrigerator overnight at least.

Grill over hot coals or roast in the toaster oven at 350 degrees turning them over at least once, because of the soy sauce these cook very fast so watch them closely we can always add more heat we just can't take it away.

 MIKE AND STEVE SNIEZAK

Pork Ribs and Chicken

Use the same rub as in the crock pot ribs and chicken and then when they are about done (around 150 degrees if you have a probe) coat them in B.B.Q. Sauce and continue to cook until the sauce glazes over and looks hard

Country Cordon Bleu

Wrap a chicken breast in plastic or put it in a sandwich bag so you can pound it flat without making a mess, generally you can smack it with the palm of your hand to flatten it enough to roll. Remove it from the plastic lay it down flat on your cutting board, take a slice or cut a heavy strip of your favorite cheese (Swiss is commonly used) and roll it up in the middle of the chicken breast. Then take a strip of bacon and wrap this around the chicken breast like a string and taking a few tooth picks stick them through the whole thing to hold it together. Make up as many of these as you want and then bake them for about 20 minutes at 350 degrees, (unless it's low and slow everything is at 350 degrees) until the cheese just starts to melt out, same on the grill.

Roast Reds

Cut 3 or 4 red potatoes in quarter pieces put them in a bowl drizzle on some olive oil, sprinkle with sea salt paprika and a little nutmeg mix this all together and spread them on a cookie sheet to bake for about 45 minutes as a side dish. For a meal add diced bacon or ham, onions and bell pepper, you can grill this to you just need a pan or something to hold them.

Zucchini or Yellow Squash

Cut off the ends and slice each squash down the middle, one large squash is a good side dish.

Coat the cut side with Italian dressing and lay the squash skin side down on the grill or skin side down on a cookie sheet to roast it in the oven. On the grill turn it over after about five minutes and when it is soft but not mushy to the touch it is done. In the oven about ten minute will do and keep in mind vegetables can be eaten raw so it is better to under cook them a bit rather than over cooking them.

Resting

Resting is most notably done with steaks but I have found it applies to almost everything heck even oatmeal is better rested. What this means and I will use steak as an example is once the steak is cooked to where you want it which should be a little under done from where you like it. You than place the steak off to the side to rest for about ten minutes (the guru's say 20 minutes but come on I am hungry already). This not only allows the tissues of the meat to relax making it tenderer but it will continue to cook briefly. To illustrate this point I will use prime rib (yummy) a medium rare prime rib is about 145 degrees Fahrenheit because of the large size of a whole prime rib I will rest it for about 30 minutes, so I only cook it to around 115 degrees I then set it off to the side where it is warm but not hot and in about 30 minutes it is around 145 degrees and very, very tender. This is where our planning comes in, the next time you bake a turkey for the holidays plan to start it an hour earlier then you normally would and when the turkey is cooked to where you like it leave it in the oven but turn the oven off and just crack open the oven door a little so some of the heat can get out let that old bird just hang out in that warm oven for an hour before serving it and see if it doesn't fall off the bone.

Steak 101

Turn your hand palm side up and with a finger of your other hand gently poke your palm from the center towards the base of your thumb. The center of your palm represents what well done steak feels like while the base of your thumb represents what rare steak feels like and the area in-between represents the various temperatures. If you want a well done steak take it off the grill or out of the oven when it is medium well, if you want a medium rare steak take it off the grill or out of the oven when it is a little past rare and rest it. Steak cooking is more art than science and many of us are simply not gifted such as myself where as our Gal Sal can cook a steak just the way you want it while doing her nails and surfing the net...of coarse she is our Gal Sal just the same if you screw up a few steaks don't panic the beauty of feeding yourself alone on the road is no one is there to hear you cry...It also means you have plenty of time to practice so the next time you grill for a group they will all be in awe.

I don't season my steaks, just don't care for them that way I don't use steak sauce either just knock off their horns wipe their ass and send them out and if you are cooking steaks for a group I suggest you do the same just make sure there is plenty of sauce and seasoning on the table people are very picky when it comes to their beef and if you take on the responsibility of feeding them you better be ready for the grief. That being said my buddy the mighty Quinn is what I call a 5 star country cook, he just has a common sense about him when it comes to country cooking and what Quinn does with steak is a brief marinade.

Steak Quinn Style

For 1 large steak

Lay the steak in a pan deep enough to cover the steak

Sprinkle a light coating of your favorite seasoning on the steak, (Montreal rocks)

Now coat the steak with a layer of Worcestershire sauce

Flip the steak over and back trying to coat the whole steak with this mixture

Now pour in enough water to cover the steak and let it rest for 30 minutes to an hour before grilling or baking it

What this does is it dilutes the power of the seasoning just slightly so it is not as over powering and blends the flavor together rather nicely, if I ever do eat seasoned steak this is my favorite way.

Toppings

Equal amounts of mushroom slices and onion slices in your soup bowl with a teaspoon of butter covered in the microwave for 3-5 minutes

Melt 2 teaspoons of butter in your soup bowl add a ¼ cup of cooked bay shrimp a little bay seasoning, a teaspoon of flour and mix this together add about a half cup of milk and microwave until hot and creamy stirring every few minutes

BAKING

EVERYTHING BAKES AT 350 degrees Fahrenheit...I know it doesn't but for our purposes it does. You can also bake breads real well in your crock pot the down side is that it ties up the pot for most of the day, also the Chief pointed out yesterday that his toaster oven is not high enough for a loaf of bread to rise and bake in...we can get around that. High gluten or bread flour makes a great loaf of bread but we don't have the room to carry all this extra stuff so all purpose flour will do it just makes a loaf that is a little denser and does not rise as high which will work here for our purposes nicely.

Yeast notes; Keep your yeast refrigerated or in a very cool place it does not like heat. Always start your yeast by adding it to warm water, not hot with the sugar for about 5 minutes or until it has bubbled up. If the recipe does not call for sugar add just a pinch this is what yeast feeds on and it needs it to get going.

Basic Bread

This is my own variation on a simple bread, I have reduced the size of the recipe as far as I can but it still makes a healthy sized loaf so what I do at home is after the first rise I break it up into 4 balls of dough, bake one and freeze the others by rubbing them down lightly with oil and putting them one at a time into sandwich bags. You can then as an example take the frozen dough ball out of the freezer pull it out of the bag and put it into your crock pot that you have sprayed with pan spray, put it on low cover it and when you smell fresh bread it is done… again this will tie up your crock pot for a good 6 hours or more so if you can thaw the dough ball and let it rise and bake it in the oven then do so, just the same ¼ of this recipe made into a loaf of bread is a nice size loft for one for one meal…fresh baked bread…on the road…come on, who's going to say no to that?

1 cup of warm water not hot

Stir in one tablespoon of sugar

Stir in 1 tablespoon or one package of yeast

Set this off to the side for 5 minutes or until it bubbles a little

In a large bowl, (if you don't have one then use the pot from your crock pot)

3 cups of flour

1 teaspoon sea salt

1 tablespoon melted or soft butter, (butter gives bread a crispy crust, for softer bread use vegetable or olive oil in the same amount)

1 egg

Add the water, sugar, yeast mix and mix together

You can start mixing this with a spoon if you want but it is dough and sooner or later you will have to man handle it, (pardon the pun)

Gloves won't work here because the dough will stick to them. Wash your hands and then after you dry them try to cover them with flour this will help to keep some of the dough from sticking to your fingers. Regardless as the dough becomes dough it will hold together by itself so just keep kneading the dough with your hands and in time you will have a nice ball. If the dough stays to wet add more flour a little at a time, if to dry add water a little at a time. This is where dough making becomes art and you just have to feel your way through it, what you want in the end is a ball of dough like play dough but just a little tacky.

Cover the bowl of dough with a towel or some sort of cover allowing the gasses to escape but not allowing the dough to dry out, now let it rise until double in size or about 1 hour.

Punch the dough down knocking the air out of it and tear it into 4 equal parts rolling each into a ball, take 3 of these and rubbing them with oil lightly store them as mentioned above.

Take one ball and place it on a well greased baking sheet then push it down about halfway making a flat loaf, then covering it with a towel let it rise again for about an hour or until it is roughly the size you want. Now here is where we deal with the issue of narrow toaster ovens, you can actually bake the bread right now it does not have to rise a second time the second rise helps the bread to be more fluffy so if you bake it now it will be a bit more dense but if you are dipping it into beans or something this may be better for you…regardless just let it rise to the size where it will still fit in the oven and remember it will rise a little more in the oven.

Your bread is done when you smell it, when it is G.B.D., and when you thump the top and it feels sort of like thumping a melon…sort of, solid is what I mean about 20 minutes

Cornbread

This is a thick batter somewhat like pancakes but a little thicker and again it can be left a little lumpy which will help it to rise and be fluffy. This best bakes in a cast iron skillet and if you really like the idea of cooking on the road I really suggest you look into cast iron, it really is the best. This can also be baked in your crock pot on high for about 2 hours not so bad, or what I like to do is when making beans or such in the crock pot I will pour this over the top of the beans in the last hour or so of cooking and get a big cornbread dumpling…and if you are trucking somewhere through the cold, cold north I guarantee that a dish like that will warm you up, fill you up, and brighten your day.

¾ cup of flour

½ cup corn meal

1/3 cup of sugar

2 teaspoons of baking powder

1good pinch of sea salt

¾ cup of butter milk, (if you don't have butter milk regular milk is fine, I have even done this with water…I just think butter milk is best)

1 egg

3 teaspoon of vegetable oil

2 teaspoons of melted butter

Mix together and pour into a well greased pan, bake for about 20 minutes or until the top browns and the sides pull away from the walls and the center thump is solid

Options

Mix in a small handful of sliced canned jalapenos for an added kick, also it is no sin to run with Jiffy mix cornbread this is a fine product and is basically the dry ingredients from above, you can bake it as directed or jazz it up with butter milk and a little butter…whatever works for you…I just like mine better…

Basic Biscuits

Biscuit dough is gooey, sticky, and messy also you really can't make one or two at a time. For ease and convince I suggest either canned raw biscuits or frozen raw biscuits each are fine products and will save you hassle, just the same as Mac Daddy would say, "Anything worth doing is worth over doing."

In a large salad sized bowl mix the following

1 ¾ cups of flour

½ teaspoon sea salt

1 tablespoon (which is three teaspoons) baking powder

5 tablespoons of vegetable shortening or vegetable oil

¾ cup milk

Mix this together and roll it out on a floured surface then cut it into biscuits with a cup or can or biscuit cutter...or just drop big fat spoonfuls onto a baking sheet and bake for 7-10 minutes again when they are golden brown they are done.

Pizzas!

There is not much more out there that makes me sick then paying $20.00 or more for a pizza that has about $5.00 worth of stuff on it especially when I can make it fresh on the road.

This will make about 4 personal pizzas; again feel free to freeze the extra dough.

Prepare your yeast

>   Into 2 cups of warm water (not hot)

>   1 tablespoon or 1 package of yeast

>   1 pinch of sugar

>   Let stand for 5 minute or until a little bubbly

>   3 ½ cups of flour

>   ¼ cup olive oil

>   ½ teaspoon of sea salt

Water, yeast, flour, oil, and salt…that is all there is to pizza dough…the rule of fives was never explained more elegantly, basically all you need to make any given dish is five ingredients anymore and you take away from the dish…Now this is more philosophy than function, but the concept remains the same.

Mix her all together and let it rise just like the basic bread recipe, then punch it down and form four balls for mini pizzas or if you have room in the oven or grill you can use the whole ball or half regardless the rest remains the same.

Trying to avoid the need to carry a rolling pin simply pound the ball of dough flat and then start pulling it out by holding it in front of you by the upper edge and turning it like the steering wheel of your truck through your hands letting the weight of the dough pull it down. When you have the desired thickness and size you want lay it on a baking sheet for the oven or lightly greased piece of tin foil for the grill, then taking your fork poke little holes all over the top of the pizza. What this does is keeps it from rising unevenly when baking or proofing, now put in the oven for about 5-10 minutes we don't really want to bake it all the way we just want to seal the dough so the sauce does not make it mushy. For the grill we are only using the tin foil to keep it from sticking so lay the dough foil down on the grill for about five minute and then flip it keeping it on the foil or using the foil to roll it onto another piece of foil bake for about another five minute and remove.

Sauce

K.I.S.S. I have seen insane things done with sauce and it is just sad, first of all if you are a fan of some premade spaghetti sauce and you carry it with you for your own spaghetti night then just use that the only secret to saucing a pizza is keep it thin, too much sauce and things slide off. As for tradition and invoking the rule of five, basic marinara is simply plain tomato sauce with olive oil and basil where as basic pizza sauce is marinara with oregano added and again I emphasize basic as in the starting point but I have seen self empowered chef's using 15 plus ingredients to make a pizza sauce that you are going to cover with cheese and other ingredients...where is the logic there?

For your own sauce I like tomato puree but for ease and storage

> 1 small can of tomato sauce (if using all the dough a soup can size will probably do)

2 shots of olive oil

1 teaspoon dry basil

1 teaspoon dry oregano

1 teaspoon granulated garlic

Mix this together cold it does not need to be cooked, spread sauce onto the pizzas using a spoon or something flat to spread it out like butter on bread.

Sprinkle on a thin layer of Mozzarella cheese and top with a bunch of pepperoni keeping those in a single layer, then a little more cheese just to glue everything together.

Bake until the cheese is bubbly and starting to brown about 15-20 minutes, on the grill you can now lay the pizza directly on the grill without it sticking and when the cheese melts you are there. Remember these ingredients are all ready cooked or eatable so you don't have to cook anything you just need to get it hot and melted and actually if you wish to put together the other pizzas and freeze them you can bake those in the microwave later in the week.

What was presented here was a basic pepperoni pizza which is by far the most popular...but not the only one. This is your pizza make it your own, just remember the structure poke little holes in the dough to keep it from baking unevenly, proof your dough on the grill or in the oven to shorten overall baking time and make sure the dough is baked well, keep your sauce thin so stuff does not slide off, use a little cheese on top to glue things in place and if you make a yucky pizza don't panic just make a note of it so you don't do it again.

Deep Dish

If you are on the fence about cast iron allow me to push you off, take a cast iron skillet and spray it well with pan spray. Take a ball of dough from above that has been stretched roughly into a pizza and laying into the skillet form it into the bottom of the skillet and part way up the sides, poke hole in the dough with your fork and proof it in the oven or on the grill, spread a thin layer of sauce, then cheese, then just go crazy and fill the skillet about half way with whatever you want, top with a little more cheese and bake or grill as above.

Now then, I have been working on this book for months and here in the last pages I have finally made myself drool, I need something to eat...I'll be right back...

Calzones

Pizza tacos that's all they are, lay out your stretched out dough then sauce it as above, on one half lay out your cheese and toppings, take the other half and fold it over the toppings half. Pinch the edges together to seal them poke a few holes in it with the tip of a knife so it doesn't blow up and bake it until you see stuff wanting to bubble out of the holes...simple.

Pancakes and Waffles

As mentioned back in the breakfast section there are pancake mixes that are basically the dry ingredients and all you need to do is add water most of these are affordable and not bad, but if you want the real deal here we go. Also waffles are pancakes with a little more oil and eggs added so if using a bag mix just add one egg and a tablespoon of vegetable oil for about every 2 waffles.

For pancakes this makes about 3 good sized ones

> ½ cup of milk
>
> 2 tablespoons melted butter
>
> 1 egg
>
> 1 cup of flour
>
> 2 teaspoons of baking powder
>
> 2 tablespoons of sugar
>
> ½ teaspoon of salt

Mix it all together and there you go just remember for thick fluffy pancakes and waffles leave this a little lumpy. For waffles simply add to the above;

> ¼ teaspoon of baking soda
>
> 1 egg
>
> 1 tablespoon of vegetable oil

Oh and always make sure your waffle iron is well oiled

A FEW FOR THE ROAD

As I wind this up and point myself towards the next horizon I am going to leave you with two sweet treats and two dishes I enjoy…well as you can tell I enjoy them all.

Apple Crisp

Spray the inside of your crock pot, I don't recommend a liner for this one as it would make it difficult to serve.

Pour in a can of apple pie filling…or

Slice three nice apples don't worry about peeling them unless you really need to and put them in the crock pot

Cover them with a nice layer of sugar

Dust that layer of sugar with a light layer of cinnamon, nutmeg, and ground cloves (if you have them)

Now a very light sprinkling of corn starch (this will make the juice thick as it cooks) add ¼ cup of water

Topping

Melt a stick of butter in your soup bowl

Into this mix 1 tablespoon (or 3 teaspoons) brown sugar

Add about 1 cup of raw oatmeal or enough to make thick goo

Options, you can also add a teaspoon of vanilla if you have it or maybe some chopped nuts

Pack this goop onto the apple pie filling or apple mix, cover and bake for a few hours again when you smell it and its bubbly it's ready

Snicker doodles

I have cut this recipe in half but it still makes a lot of cookies so here again as space allows you can freeze the dough and use it later. I picked this for two reasons one for me this is comfort food and for anybody that has a mom as cool as mine these may be comfort food for you to. The second reason is that I am sick and tired of seeing so called chef's that can't even make a cookie because they don't grasp the simplest of concepts. Do you recall when we talked about the butter and oil while making bread? Oil will make you bread fluffy while butter will give you a crispy crust, same concept with cookies, if you have ever seen cookies come out flat thin and kind of see through it's because there is too much butter and not enough oil. So in my cookies I don't use any butter unless I have to and this is a perfect example, my mom and sisters will blend the shortening and butter and make these awesome but that's because they are my mom and my sisters and can bake better than I can but try these and tell me they don't rock!

½ cup of shortening (you can use vegetable oil but shortening is best)

¾ cup of sugar

1 egg

1 ¼ cups of flour (you may need a little more in the end to make it tacky but firm)

1 teaspoon cream of tartar

½ teaspoon baking soda

Pinch of sea salt

Mix this altogether and roll into little balls about half the size of a golf ball, in a separate bowl combine 2 teaspoons of sugar with 1 teaspoon of cinnamon then roll the top of each ball in this and place them on the cookie sheet, bake 8-10 minutes. These cookies will puff up while baking and then fall flat when cool.

A couple of things to note I have made these using Splenda instead of sugar very successfully and acceptable for diabetics, although again consult your doctor. Also if it's easier on you self rising flour can be used in which case leave out the cream of tartar, baking soda, and salt.

Basic Pickled Eggs

The point of this is to show you how insanely easy some of this stuff is

Make enough hard boiled eggs (cover whole eggs in a pan with water and bring to a boil, boil for 5 minutes and set aside to cool. Once cool peel them under cool running water) to fill a 1 quart Mason jar, peel them and fill the jar with them.

In another pot bring 3 cups of water and 1 cup of white vinegar to a boil then remove from the heat add 2 tablespoons of Pickling spice to the water, allow to stand for 10 minutes and then pour over eggs making sure all the eggs are covered adding more water if needed. Place uncovered jar in the refrigerator to cool. Once it is cool cover tightly and refrigerate for 2 weeks...and that is all there is to it. Now you can add onions, or peppers to the eggs and pour the water mix over them, you can fill the jar with fresh vegetables instead of eggs and pour the same water mix over them, let you mind soar and enjoy your time on earth as we all should.

Salt Cured Salmon

Funny for a guy who is anti salt I close with this but if you enjoy a dried fish that is not too dry this is a good one and fairly healthy…sort of…

In a shallow pan large enough to hold a salmon filet, cover the bottom of the pan with a thin layer of sea salt. Lay the filet skin side down if skin is still present onto the salt if filet is skinless more the better. Rub a thin layer of liquid smoke onto the raw salmon followed by a thin layer of dill weed, fresh if possible but dry works fine; finally cover the salmon with another thin layer of sea salt seal the pan with plastic or a cover and refrigerate for 5 days. The fish will be covered in water by then which is good, remove the fish from the salt and rinse the salt off the fish you may have to rub it a bit but the more you remove the less salty the taste. Slice the salmon into thin strips and enjoy, goes well with the Chiefs Bachelor Buffett… which come to think of it was my mom's original "Sunshine Plate"…thanks mom! Good with bagels and cream cheese for breakfast as well.

SHOPPING LIST EXAMPLE

Meats	Grains	Dairy	Veggie/ Fruit	Non Food Items

Notes:

STORE COMPARISON EXAMPLE

Store	Food & Cost	Equip & Cost	Diabetic Needs	Blood Press Needs
Wal-Mart				
Dollar Store				

K-Mart				
Target				
Safeway				
Roth's				

Piggly-Wiggly				

Notes:

Calm seas and clear horizons to you…

Uncle Steve, Houston, Texas winter 2012

Printed in the USA
CPSIA information can be obtained
at www.ICGtesting.com
CBHW070051290624
10768CB00044B/184